BEING PUBLIC

Jeroen Boomgaard
Rogier Brom
Anke Coumans
Florian Cramer
Eva Fotiadi
Maaike Lauwaert
Gabriel Lester
Barbara Neves Alves
Steven ten Thije

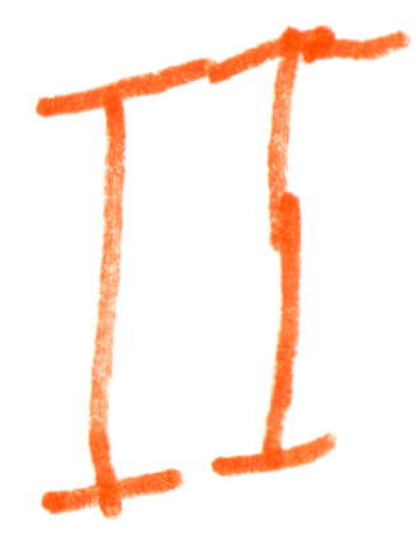

Making Public
Valiz

BEING PUBLIC
How Art Creates the Public

Jeroen Boomgaard
& Rogier Brom

(eds.)

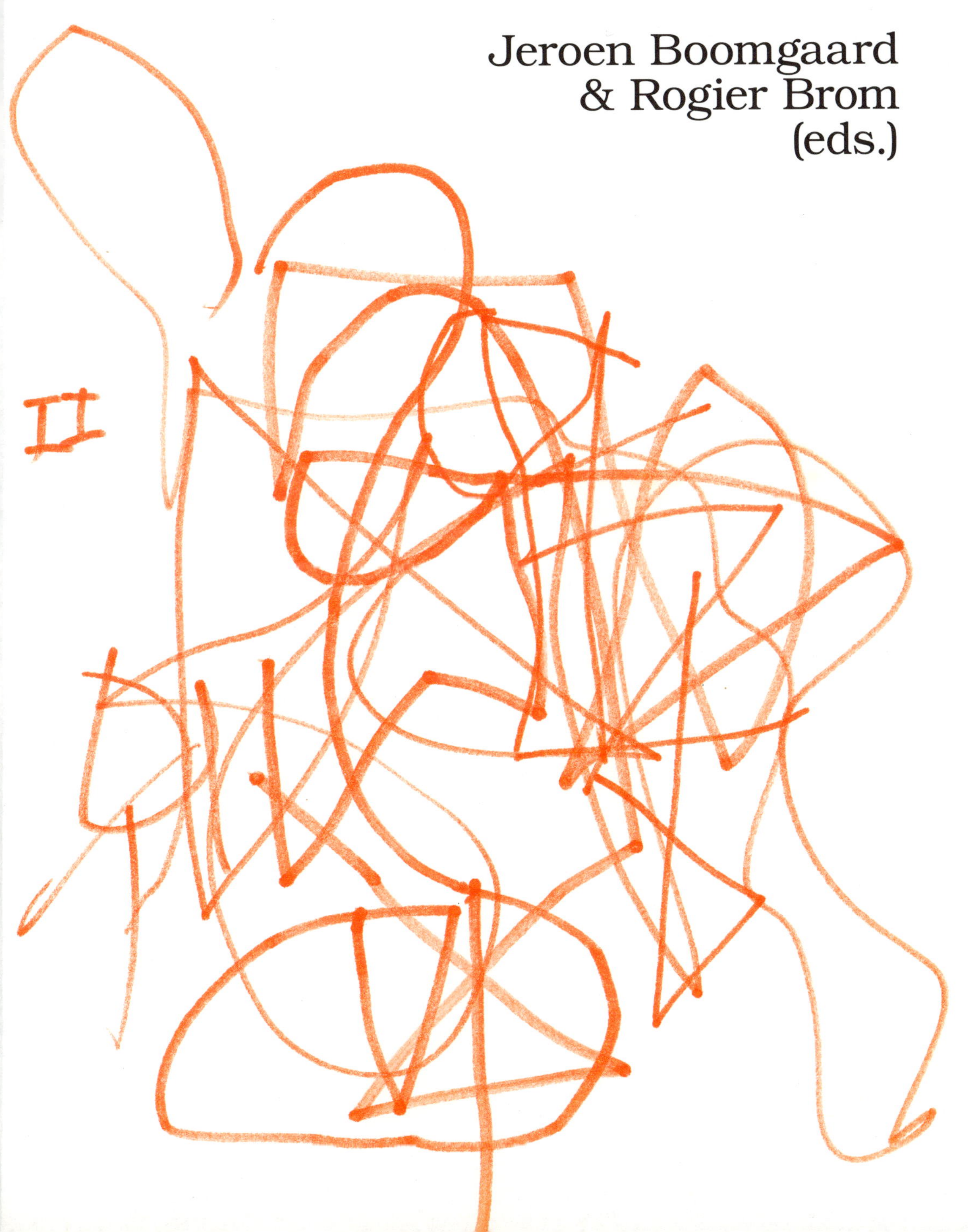

BEING PUBLIC

CONTENTS

CONTENTS

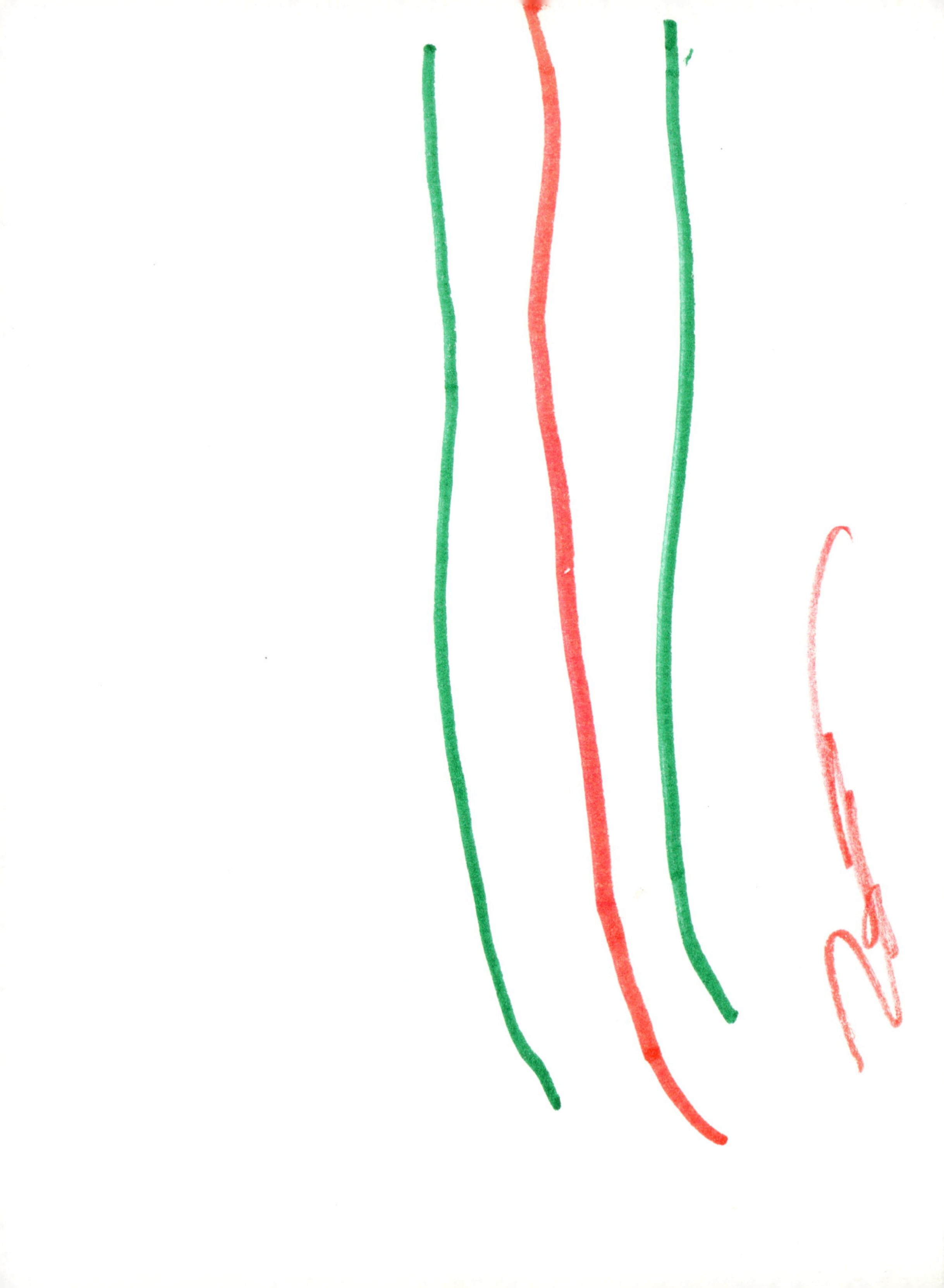

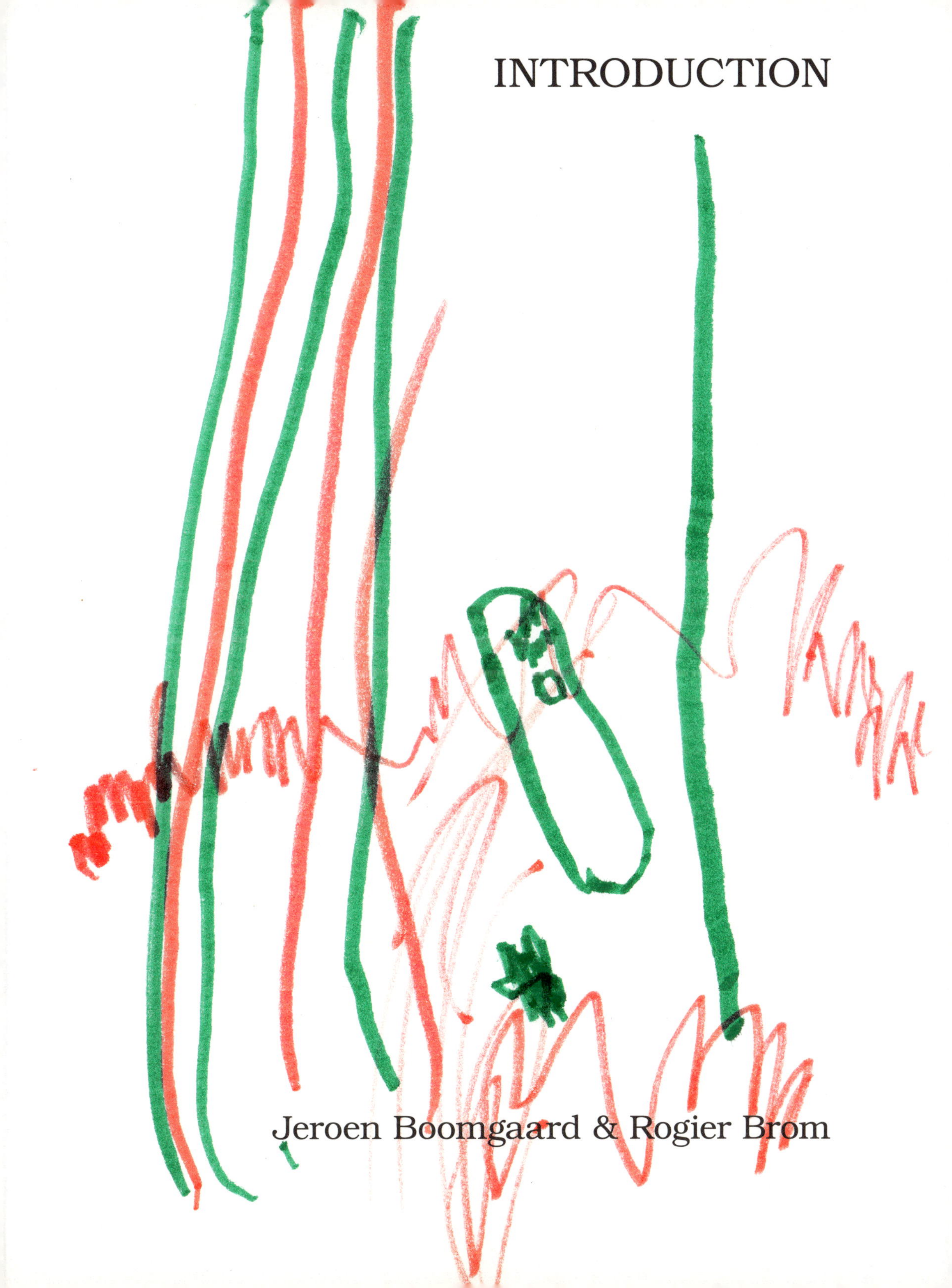

INTRODUCTION
Jeroen Boomgaard & Rogier Brom

In his contribution to the publication accompanying Skulptur Projekte Münster of 1997, Daniel Buren states that almost all sculptures that he sees outdoors are boring and toothless. They are either so generic that no one can take offence or so inconspicuous that only highly trained art historians can understand them and everyone else simply walks by without noticing them. According to Buren, one of the main causes of this sorry state of affairs is that politicians don't show enough guts in commissioning art works for the public space. However, what Buren observes here is part of a much larger problem that stems from a shift in the notion of what 'public' is. Both the public—a group of people focusing their attention on something—and the public domain, i.e. the space that we share with others without hindrance, are judged quantitatively these days. An exhibition is only a success if it draws huge crowds and the public space is deemed successful especially when it is used on a massive scale without incurring damage.

One of the consequences of this emphasis on a quantitative approach is that the notion of public loses its specificity, and domains that used to be separate in function and use are now beginning to blend. The art space is becoming more of a public space, while the public space rather becomes a space for a public to attend or participate in events and demonstrations. In this collection of essays we are not so much concerned with how these spaces are merging or with the policies that encourage and promote this development. Rather, we aim to explore, from a variety of perspectives, how art as actor in Latour's sense operates in this new, hybrid space. In all the contributions to this publication art is discussed as a phenomenon that is defined by certain spatial conditions and public expectations, but also as a presence that claims a particular space and originates a particular public.

Thus, in this book art serves as a catalyst for getting a grip on the complex whole of diverging and converging notions of the public and the public space. Because what is actually going on in this exchange between the public spaces and the closed spaces for a public? Both are legitimized by the presence of people but increasingly these people are seen as consumers. They must be triggered to gather in large numbers in one place in order to legitimize its public character. This means that the emphasis is on an offering that is potentially appealing to as many people as possible. The increase in blockbusters in museums and of 'fun' art in the street—as different as they may be—shows that event and entertainment are the driving forces of this programming. At the same time, art that emphatically rejects this development by retreating into isolation or by an appeal to singularity gets caught up in this confusion about what 'the public' is, too. In this publication, however, we try to avoid the fatalism by which isolation or surrender are presented as opposites, as if there were no other choice, by focusing on forces that

are intrinsic to art. The considerations
presented here discuss the capability
of art works to bring about a different
distribution of the sensory (Rancière),
to create new political space and space
for politics, to explore other forms of
public and to look for new publics.

The contributions in this volume deal
with the following subjects: Art and its
public (Lauwaert, Boomgaard, Brom,
Lester); the personal, the public and the
political (Ten Thije, Coumans, Fotiadi);
public behaviour and public domain
(Cramer, Neves Alves). *Being Public: How
Art Creates the Public* is about the notions
of the public and the public domain,
notions that we use frequently without
thinking too much about their meaning.
The book gives no definitions for these
terms and doesn't supply any answers,
but it does provide new insights and
it poses questions about the practices
that take place behind these terms.

HIGH EXPECTATIONS, HIGHER THRESHOLDS

Maaike Lauwaert

This essay looks at the audience conundrum in the art world from the perspective of expectations held by both arts organizations and audiences and the strange lure of high thresholds in the art world. It is written from the perspective of someone—me—who workings for an arts organization and has seen the dynamics of audience reach at work from up close.

Clichés and Fruitless Oppositions

This publication starts from the observation that audience— basically a container concept—has become a dominant factor in the discussion of the role and position of the arts. We, as a sector, are as good and as indispensable as the number of people who visit us, who take selfies in front of our exhibitions and who make public (read: online) claims about us. To be seen, to be publicly claimed on social media is to exist and to have value. Counting numbers is only one part of the audience conundrum the arts sector is in, another part is the online appropriation by users, also known as 'the people'.

Over the past few years, a rather fruitless opposition has been created in discussions in the Dutch media between art that is strongly focused on a public (blockbusters, pop up museums, large-scale manifestations around a clear-set topic et cetera) and autonomous art striving for and defending art's 'intrinsic values' (smaller exhibitions, lesser known artists et cetera). In this opposition a conflict is embedded between art that attracts huge audiences (the more the merrier! Never mind that the artworks are largely obstructed from view by throngs of people wielding selfie sticks) and art that attracts little or no audience and relies on its experimental role to validate its presence in an art space (in a laboratory, not many people are looking at the work done either, it is in the nature of the experimental game). In the first cliché setting, the audience is comprised of the masses, the large groups of people only coming out to see art when there is enough media attention and a big enough wow-factor involved. The second cliché relies on the image of a well-informed, selective and critical audience who pick and choose their art visits, carefully select where they want to be seen and sigh when hearing someone missed that one, epic, never to be repeated performance in a cellar at a friend's place. The low threshold of the blockbuster exhibition is contrasted with a threshold that cannot be high enough.

Contrary to this fruitless opposition and these cliché images often evoked in discussions and ways of thinking by both policy makers and art professionals, contemporary art audiences are in reality varied. They mix and mingle, they operate in a fragmented way, not as solid blocks of people (hence the use of the word audiences rather than audience) and they may even be unknown to institutions seeking new audiences, or are plainly invisible to them and as such audiences are very often immeasurable. Audiences also change, evolve and move about. There is no static audience and hence static approaches towards what audiences are and can be, is misleading. The reciprocity between art and audience is complex, layered and more dynamic than audience numbers and online popularity suggest.

The Problem of Expectation

What runs through most connections between art and audiences is the element of expectation. Artists or organizations try to guide, spike or beef up expectations through language used in press releases, Facebook posts and on websites but also in the images released through official channels or social media such as Instagram (which then hopefully make it onto Contemporary Art Daily). A key moment in the meeting of art and audiences (at an opening, or later when an exhibition is on view) is the question of expectations met or expectations disappointed. With the advent of websites that document exhibitions, such as CAD, the tension between the promise of an artwork and its actual manifestation increases. Brian Droitcour wrote about this issue in his article 'The Perils of Post-Internet Art' (2014) in which he defines the slippery concept of Post-Internet art in terms of its focus on online representation:

> I know Post-Internet art when I see art made for its own installation shots, or installation shots presented as art. Post-Internet art is about creating objects that look good online: photographed under bright lights in the gallery's purifying white cube (a double for the white field of the browser window that supports the documentation), filtered for high contrast and colors that pop.[1]

This created a strange sensation for Droitcour when he

> came across an installation shot of *Hhellblauu* (2008–12), a work by Kari Altmann … . In the gallery it looked like nothing … . It did nearly nothing to attract my attention …; it was just an inexpertly assembled installation by an artist who made more compelling work online. But when I saw the documentation I did a double take. The colors in the image—especially the sky blue named in the title—were intensely vibrant compared to the dull ones I remembered. The water in the pool seemed to create a viscous distance between the floating prints and the base upon which the pool rested, a platform that had looked flat when I saw it in person.[2]

What Droitcour describes is not only an issue at play with Post-Internet art but a dynamic between representation and expectation that we see across the art world. It happens in relation to press releases creating such high expectations that journalists are disappointed almost by default, by information texts saying one thing and an exhibition showing another. It is part of the whole system of how we run organizations and try to attract press attention and physical

[1] Droitcour 2014.

[2] Ibid.

visitors. And in all honesty, the fact that sometimes two exhibitions exist, one in the words and images published online and sent into the world via an *e-flux* announcement, for example, and one in a barely visited gallery space, is often not a problem at all. We get more eyeballs on the Internet than in real life, why not show ourselves from our best side for those audiences, even if it means puffing our feathers and being tempted by hyperbole?

We could say that in these expectations, on both sides, there is a certain idea or even ideal of what is the right way to look at the artworks, to understand and present them. 'The audience should get this or that reference.' 'The artist should know that people will think this or that.' All of this remains largely unspoken. But it is a very determining element in the complex negotiations between how art is presented and how it is perceived. On a social level, there is the promise of a must-see show, of something not to be missed if you want to in with the in-crowd. Fear Of Missing Out rules in our sector, after all. Luckily for those short on time or money for traveling, websites such as CAD are now an acceptable reference: 'I saw it online, it looked good!'

Frustrating Expectations

Besides being simply disappointed, audiences can break the unspoken 'contract' of participation, and frustrate expectations. On the most basic level, audiences can do this by not showing up, a very exasperating act for art institutions struggling to reach as many people as possible. Audiences may also decide not to participate in a participative show. Not to write any thoughts or ideas on that huge white wall, leaving the staff and artist to fill the space themselves in order to avoid the shame of explicit and conscious non-participation. (I was recently at an exhibition where the artist invited audience members to hold her artworks. As soon as someone refused, she was lost and the whole atmosphere collapsed. In that simple act of keeping his arms folded, this person had pulled the plug and the magic was gone. Such is the power of audiences). Audiences can refrain from posting on Facebook and Instagram, a more silent protest against an exhibition that did not meet the social media standards of interestingness, funniness, or selfie-ness.

New Audiences

Stepping away from this quantifiable relationship between art, art organizations and audiences in which visitors, users, tweeters et cetera can be counted (and these numbers often can and will be monetized), there is a harder to measure relationship between audiences and art works in which art becomes part of the viewers' shared or individual fabric of experiences, as French philosopher Jacques Rancière calls it.[3] In this fabric we are not alone, according to Rancière: 'The solitude of the artwork is a false solitude.' What the artist does, writes Rancière, is 'weave a new sensory fabric' by altering the 'fabric of common experience' and by weaving this new fabric, 'creating a form of common expression, or a form of expression of the community, namely "the song of the earth or the cry of men".'[4]

Commonality is created in and through art experiences that take us out of the everyday, that tear holes in the fabric of the ordinary, whether we experience these art works as a group or individually. Not only does art create a (new) fabric of experiences, it also creates (new) audiences by bringing people together around a (temporary) shared interest or activity. These new audiences do not arise out of thin air; they are assembled, reassembled and created from a breeding ground of interests, beliefs and serendipities.

Here the work of American sociologist Mark Granovetter on collective behaviour, tipping points and thresholds may be helpful.[5] We often assume that collective behaviour is based on similar individual decisions. With riots, for example, it is often assumed that each individual rioter comes to the decision to riot. Granovetter showed, however, that we are all driven by our own thresholds, some of us will start a riot, others will follow when a small group is

3
Rancière 2008.

4
Ibid.

5
Granovetter 1978.

already active, and still others only when huge numbers of people are rioting. Only when our personal threshold is reached, do we do something we would not normally do. Rioters are therefore a heterogeneous group.

However, with the in-crowd art audience sketched in one of the two clichés above, something strange is going on: the fewer people go somewhere, in other words the more exclusive something is, the more attractive it becomes. The threshold cannot be high enough. But for the vast majority of audiences and for those people who are not yet part of our audiences, a different high threshold is at work. They need a vast majority of people to lead the way in order to dare cross a threshold. The complexity of how art institutions operate is that with every public event, energy is geared towards unleashing 'a riot', that is, bringing together more people than you expected, creating momentum in the present moment but also in aftershocks on online platforms.

Journalist Malcolm Gladwell adapts the theory of Granovetter in an interesting way: why don't we consider certain collective events as slow-motion, endlessly evolving riots whereby the actions of each new participant make sense only in relation and in response to what previously took place?[6] In other words, and looked at from the troubled perspective of art audiences—what drives them and how we can reach them—why not regard visiting an art institution as a slow, sluggish and changing wave of people, interests and the building of a collective fabric?

The high threshold of the art world is a double one: for some audiences it is the reason they participate (exclusivity is what attracts them), for others it is what keeps them away. By focusing on the ongoing movement of audiences rather than trying to attract new audiences with every event, by accepting that there is no static audience but rather a varied mix of fragmented groups that change, evolve and move about, by being aware of the expectations you create, art spaces might solve part of the audience conundrum and adapt their communication strategies accordingly, whether

6
Gladwell 2015.

they are promoting a blockbuster show or a small-scale experimental exhibition.

The key is keeping on the right side of being over-eager to please, being too generous with hyperbole, being too focused on new audiences and not seeing the audiences that are already there, in short: staring too much at the numbers and failing to see the fabric of experiences that is being woven.

PUBLIC AS PRACTICE

Jeroen Boomgaard

What does it actually mean to belong to a public? Strangely enough, this question is hardly addressed in publications about the issue of the public. Public is never approached from an individual perspective, but is always seen as a group, as an undifferentiated mass that must be segmented, reached and serviced in order to let the cultural market function. However, those discussing the issue rarely seem to be a part of that real potential public themselves. In this article, by contrast, I will attempt to study the public from that personal perspective. Obviously, this attempt is doomed to fail, since I, as a professional beholder, am 'hors publique': I am supposed to observe everything with interest, to always be there without being actually involved. That I will nonetheless attempt to explore the public from a personal point of view is because I wish to find out how the individual and the general are intertwined when one is part of a public, and how this relates to the confusion between the private and the public that is characteristic of public space nowadays. In the course of this exploration I will inevitably move on from my own experience to that of a supposed group-bound 'I'.

Today, the public is more present than ever before. It is not only one of the main elements that determine the policies of governments and art institutes, but is more massively present than ever before, both physically and virtually. Museums and other art institutes are expected to go to extremes in order to reach out to a 'different' public. Highly educated, grey-haired people no longer suffice: the intended target group is young, poly-cultural and unskilled. And more than ever, museums use all possible means, from a multitude of social media to logistic operations, to bring in this potential public. Such efforts also affect programming. Thinking in terms of target groups implies that they differ in their preferences and that this should be taken into account if they are to be reached.

These target groups usually are rather vaguely defined in socio-cultural terms: they are defined by a combination of chance and choice. Unwished-for economic circumstances go hand-in-hand with self-selected spending patterns, which makes it difficult to decide how best to approach such groups. Following the Belgian philosopher Isabelle Stengers, I will call these different groups forming as many publics 'practices', because attracting these potential publics can only succeed if one manages to relate to the manner in which they regard their being-a-public as part of their practice. After all, before I visited that specific exhibition in that particular museum, I was already part of a certain public, since I was willing to go to an exhibition, or to go and see that artwork. The practice that determines that I am or will be that public is primarily formed by upbringing and education and is embedded in other forms and activities, in a complex whole of choices and habits, places and presences, that play a part in my decision to go and look at art in that place, and at that moment. As Stengers stresses, it is a practice to which I belong, not one I am a part of. The distinction lies in the overarching, passive character of the latter phrase, against the active, conscious one of the former.[1] This is not about consuming, at least it cannot be reduced to that, but about an act, a choice, an activity. By belonging to a certain public practice I, as public, am an a priori 'we', because otherwise I would not have been there at that moment at all. A practice comes with rules and responsibilities, it allows me to do, understand and produce things. Or not to do them, or to neglect them, without leaving that practice behind. If we regard being-public as part of a certain practice, we also understand how we can be an art public without actually visiting a museum or theatre. We regard the mere possibility to make use of these cultural facilities as part of our practice and this co-determines our preference for where to live, as was shown in Gerard Marlet's study.[2]

A major part of the current policy of museums can be understood as an attempt to become part of public practices that do not naturally include museums in their

[1] Stengers 2005a, pp. 190–91.

[2] Marlet 2009.

domain. Seen from this perspective, it also becomes clear why museums spread their activities in such a manner that they sometimes resemble shops, coffee bars or restaurants more than places where art is paramount. We cannot simply dismiss the motives for this as commercial gain or a neglect of core tasks: these are elements that belong to certain practices, practices that can be stretched by making looking at art part of the experience of shopping, drinking a café latte and having a nice dinner. By transforming themselves into less unequivocal places, by becoming nodes of practices, museums of contemporary art succeed in hosting other practices too: one can now visit a museum of modern art without immediately regarding oneself as its public.

Public Practices

What kind of public am I outside the museum? In what way is art in the public domain part of my practice? Or perhaps the question should be: in what way can art in the public domain be part of existing practices? Because whereas it is clear that in the museum a number of different practices come together, the public in public space is by definition indeterminate. There is no specific public for these artworks, which have to fend for themselves without the benefit of a clear framework. It is this vagueness that makes it difficult for artists to clearly place their work and drives commissioning bodies to distraction because they don't really know whether the work they have commissioned will be embraced, tolerated, ignored or rejected.

This was not always so. Just as the museum for modern art was once for everyone without being accountable for whether anyone actually came, art in public space used to lead a carefree existence in the belief that it benefited the common good. After this general visual language was exposed as the representation of the self-interest of the ruling class, a lot changed. The public no longer consists of an unstructured collection of individuals but, in the public domain as in the museum, of specific groups that all require a specific approach. But whereas in the museum it is a matter of bringing these groups together by creating an environment and providing a programme that meets their wishes, in public space it is art itself that must adapt to certain places and communities. Over the past few decades, the public domain has been subdivided into ever more intricate zones and areas with specific aims or characteristics. And the artworks take their place in this. While the inner cities are for festivals and spectacular landmark artworks that should convince visitors of the cultural value of the city, in the residential areas outside the centre the needs of the population must be met by more accessible art. And in underprivileged neighbourhoods—euphemistically renamed 'power neighbourhoods' in the Netherlands—the focus is on projects that foreground social participation and co-creation.

However, such emphatic localizing and territorializing appear to become less and less necessary. Social media now enable us to continue our shared practices anywhere, anytime. All we need is an available network. But this virtual practice, which is neither completely private nor fully public and so clearly demonstrates that the core of the We-feeling, of the choices and responsibilities that come with belonging to a certain practice, cannot escape from the physical environment that I perforce share with others: other individuals, groups and practices. Where I live, work, do my shopping and go out is part of the practices to which I belong, while simultaneously shaping them.

Stengers advocates approaching different practices from their own preferences and not gauge them by general values that either belittle them or force them onto the defensive. She specifically opposes enlightenment operations aimed at eliciting hidden or suppressed creative forces.[3] Many current social practices are facing this reproach, and I will come back to that later. An agenda aimed at education and emancipation is however no longer the obvious thing. More and more often Dutch government policy stimulates and supports art projects that aim to consolidate or

[3] Stengers 2005a, p. 187.

facilitate existing practices. The 'ecology of practices' mentioned by Stengers appears to be the guiding principle of this policy. Social cohesion, neighbourhood meetings, empowerment of the disenfranchised, but also a policy aimed at realizing artworks on the initiative of local residents, as practised by the CBK (Centre for Visual Art) in Rotterdam: it all points to reinforcing public practices as a method to enhance the quality of life in the city and make residents feel at home in a context that adapts itself to them instead of the other way around.

No matter how successful this approach may be, it does have its downsides. The ecology of practices is not all peaceful. Different public practices can severely hinder each other or even be mutually exclusive. Any policy wishing to steer things in the right direction will inevitably favour certain living habits and preferences and certain groups will be marginalized or excluded because of strategic or stealthy gentrification of certain areas. And such a policy, as Pascal Gielen observes, also results in an impoverished public domain. The confrontation with what is different, deviant and strange is increasingly avoided and we lose sight of the fundamental differences between certain practices. People living in cities are no longer questioned as to their preferences and prejudices. Because of this, not just the political dimension of the public domain is lost, as Gielen states, but one may also wonder where on this neatly ordered map of preferences and practices there is still a place for publicness, a place one could call public.[4] Within the context of the present text the main objection is that this approach robs art of its ability to bring about the openness of the society, the essential space for what is other and different.[5] To come back to the question at the beginning of this essay: in the public domain I am increasingly waited on hand and foot, but is that what I expect in my public practice?

4
Gielen 2015, p. 278.

5
For a further elaboration, see Boomgaard 2011.

Let's leave the street and return to the exhibition space. Whereas music is known for forming bonds, many forms of visual art appeal to individual experience, which makes the presence of others irksome rather than stimulating.[6] According to the Danish sculptor/installation artist Olafur Eliasson, the only thing that visitors to an exhibition have in common is that they are completely different from each other. Everyone sees and thinks something different in the encounter with an artwork, yet the entire communication strategy of the museum that displays the work is aimed at combining this multitude of experiences into the greatest common denominator. Still according to Eliasson, this means that visitors are addressed in a moralizing or patronizing manner.[7] And he is right. The minute I visit an exhibition, I am part of the public there and addressed accordingly. And this annoys me, as does the presence of others admiring the same work and saying the same thing I am saying or perhaps something altogether different. However, I doubt whether this only applies to visual art. Other art forms may be geared to receiving their public in groups and have a public that is sharing something by definition, if only by the fact that they see the same thing at the same moment at the same location. Still, the discomfort invoked by sharing an un-shareable experience is something I can also feel when attending a performance of experimental music. Much more than with classical music and also more than with exhibitions of art that has already been part of the art canon for a long time. Apparently my public practice has two sides: one that doesn't mind sharing the experience and accepts the We-feeling this evokes, and one that makes me feel uncomfortable and doesn't want to belong to a 'we'. If, based on experience, I assume that I share this not wanting to share an experience with many others, a public practice emerges that speaks to 'the individual', as opposed to a practice that gains in

6

Also see Sheikh 2015, p. 252.

7

Eliasson in a conversation with Ingo Niermann (Niermann 2011, pp. 36–37): 'The challenge for me would be to collect a bunch of data that would support the individualization of the viewer. The fact is, of course, that everyone sees something different. Everyone sees himself or herself, you could say. Not only because we think differently, we also see differently on a fundamental level … . And in the whole idea of art communication, art pedagogy, public relations—the whole notion of a museum—I would have to get used to the fact that the only common denominator there between people is that they are extremely different. I think it is possible to develop a plural language that speaks to everyone in a truly extraordinary, phenomenological way. Good artworks also do that on their own, but often the problem is that the institutions' communication efforts are so limiting or alarming that that everyone feels slightly moralized or patronized—controlled—by this extreme generalization. You could say that supporting differing perceptions is a project of individualization.'

experiential strength through massiveness (rock concerts, sunny days in the park, sports and games, parties).

Eliasson describes the individual experience as follows: 'The fact is, of course, that everyone sees something different. Everyone sees himself or herself, you could say.' He calls supporting this experience a project of individualization. Although I agree with him that we all probably see something different, I doubt whether we only have ourselves in our sights. If artworks would only be our mirrors, they couldn't have the disruptive, unsettling effect we ascribe to them. Bruno Latour is more precise in his description of what happens in our encounter with an artwork, as this larger quote shows:

> A work of art *engages* us, and if it is quite true that it has to be interpreted, at no point do we have the feeling that we are free to do 'whatever we want' with it. If the work needs a *subjective* interpretation, it is in a very special sense of the adjective: we are *subject* to it, or rather we *win* our SUBJECTIVITY through it. … Emitted by the work, such downloads allow the recipient to be moved while gradually becoming a 'friend of interpretable objects'. If listeners are gripped by a piece, it is not at all because they are projecting their own pathetic subjectivity on it; it is because the work demands that they, insignificant amateurs, brilliant interpreters, or passionate critics, become part of its *journey of instauration* – but without dictating what they must do to show themselves worthy of it.[8]

8
Latour 2013, pp. 240–41.

Becoming a subject, individualization, then is much more than simply recognizing ourselves. It is much more a process in which we become something that wasn't there before. At the risk of causing a huge conceptual confusion here and while realizing that I should present a much more elaborate exposé about these concepts that try to encapsulate what we, thrown back on ourselves, are, want, can, know and feel,

I still would like to contrast this subjectification with the We-experience that we also have or, rather, execute as part of our public practice. I don't mean to say that in this We-experience, in the choices we share with many others and in the experiences we gain in this and about which we communicate, write think and dream, we would not be subjects. Following Louis Althusser's central thesis with regard to the function of ideology, one could say that in these practices we, as part of these practices, are 'hailed as subjects'. And these days, this happens in a way and based on information about our preferences and choices that is much more elaborate than Althusser could ever have imagined. He regarded it as the basic ruse used by the dominant ideology to hide its suppressive character and make its subjects bring about their submission voluntarily.[9] The public practices I am referring to here are not purely suppressive, as they enable us to shape our lives and make us feel at home.

They did not, however, emerge fully autonomous either and in that sense the subject that is constructed in them becomes an hotchpotch of social expectations, commercial incentives, personal impulses and exchange protocols that make us part of certain communities of wishes with overlapping life patterns, fears and desires. A personal public-private construct with all of the associated problems.[10] It is precisely this constructed subject, this 'I' that places me with that artwork at that moment, which—in the confrontation with that artwork—is torn down and has to be rebuilt from scratch.

I regard this disastrous effect that artworks can have on the makeshift construction we call 'I' as the essence of the autonomy of art. It is an effect that artworks seem to lose once we are used to them: the canon puts us at ease. Still, they never quite lose all their power: every good artwork retains the ability to move me to the core time and again, to hit me there were no public practice has been established yet. However, it must be given the opportunity to do so.

9
Althusser 2001, pp. 115–18.

10
The public-private collaboration is the currently preferred way of constructing government buildings. It is a system that invites endless negotiations as all parties concerned want to have as many certainties, guarantees and windfalls as possible while the final result often brings mostly uncertainties and disappointments.

Manifestation and Misunderstanding

Outside the safe framework of the exhibition space artworks don't have much chance of exerting their disruptive powers. Lost in an undifferentiated public domain they disturb nothing and no one. It seems that art in the public space can only be saved by a policy of placing them within a certain framework, thereby connecting them to existing (public) practices in which their visibility is guaranteed. And yet this is not quite so. In a sense this emphatic embedding can become the very thing that disrupts the possible effect of art works in and for the public domain. To illustrate what this entices I will introduce the concept of manifestation. A manifestation is both the appearance of a phenomenon and a public display. Whereas the first meaning of the word stresses the moment of becoming public, the second one is more suggestive of the presence of participants, or a public. Within the framework of this text one could say that this second meaning is more in line with public practices, but the term is also quite useful to characterize the various ways in which art is brought into public space and connected to existing practices. The preference for festivals that can mobilize many people for a short period, as well as the support of small-scale participation projects in which either real or fictitious communities work together on the initiative of an artist, show that gathering a certain audience for a certain event forms an essential starting point. Of course we cannot heap together all forms of art in public space, but even the revealing of a new sculpture in a refurbished square can be regarded as a manifestation, since the square manifests itself as new. It is an event that stresses the revised role of that place within the urban fabric, the influence of government and perhaps private parties in realizing it, and, finally, the practices in which the location is being inscribed. Then and there, the artwork symbolizes at once change and a connection to the real or desired community of the neighbourhood. While in huge political manifestations people express a shared protest or resistance, these

11
Zuidervaart 2011, p. 126:
'The special contribution
of art in public is to help
people carry out their
explorations and presentations and interpretations in
an imaginative fashion, to
help them disclose in fresh
and insightful ways the felt
quality and lived experi-
ence of concerns that merit
public attention. Products
and events of art in public
that accomplish this sort
of imaginative disclosure
exemplify and foster critical
and creative dialogue both
within various publics and
among them. Such art
also presupposes that the
publics addressed, either
potentially or actually, are
not mere collections of
self-interested individuals.
The publics of art in public
are themselves internally
connected and cross-con-
nected by virtue of shared
traditions, social positioning, and patterns of interpretation that exceed and
inform the experience of
any individual member.'

organized gatherings create a shared experience and an experience of sharing.[11] One could also say that the careful alignment of the artwork with the wishes or needs of the residents and/or visitors makes a certain image of those wishes or needs concrete while excluding everything that deviates from them. Specific, unwanted practices are not included in the picture.

The shared experience that aims to stimulate and enhance these existing (public) practices is usually accompanied by an overdosis of communication. Only in this manner does the manifestation become coherent and generates the desired consensus. And although the embedding in existing practices is an absolute condition for the functioning of art in the public domain—without some form of recognition no form of acknowledgement is possible—the communication usually is not respectful of the artwork: the moralizing and patronizing signalled by Eliasson in the museum also applies to the public domain. And just as in an exhibition a dominant theme and smart information campaign can compel an artwork to soundlessly echo prompted wordings, the emphasis on communication with art in the public domain can render the artwork all but invisible, reducing it to no more than a vague shadow obscured by brochures filled with messages.

The trend as outlined above fits in the de-politicization of public space, as already observed by Gielen. The public domain is not something that must be established or confirmed; it is a social environment cum practice, a network of conflicts, confrontations, coalitions and constructions that is being realized over and over again, as it should be. In other words, the public domain is never designed and never to be taken for granted. Unlike with the current approach, art could be a much stronger disturbing element: the artwork as the pre-eminent deviant or other, in order to underline the constantly to be gained open character of shared space. In contrast with the view that art should convey what we have in common in order to support the public domain is Rancière's proposition that it is precisely dissensus, the disruption of what our senses are used to, that provides the opportunity for change and innovation. Rancière, who is more extensively discussed elsewhere in this publication, considers dis-identification, the fact that the artwork does not meet our expectations, a condition for any form of emancipation.[12]

Identification and confirmation of my (public) practice thus seem to be in direct opposition to denying them as a condition for being able to speak of a domain with the possibility of openness. And whereas theorists who are more concerned with the value and functioning of art generally forefront dis-identification and dis-sensus, the theory of art in the public domain, even while embracing the basic idea of dissensus, advocates a necessary re-identification. The theory argues that the individual disruption of the senses and the resulting individualization or individuation cannot lead to the solidarity and joint resistance that are a condition for changing the political balance.[13] A certain form of re-identification seems inevitable if one really intends to challenge the powers that be.

High time to illustrate this with an example. Currently, in Flanders there is a project that not only clearly demonstrates some of the dilemmas mentioned earlier but also provides an adequate response to them. In the municipality of Herzele lies the old village Ressegem, one of the numerous townlets in the Flemish countryside. It boasts the remnants of a motte-and-bailey castle, an old presbytery and some farmhouses in beautiful surroundings that are feeling the pressure of urbanization. What is special about Ressegem is that there has been a piece of common land in the centre of the village since time memorial. Plans to do something with this land have invariably led to much disagreement and have met with resistance from local residents. An initial plan to build a new town hall and a block of apartments there was

12
Rancière 2009a, pp. 72–73: 'Aesthetic experience has a political effect to the extent that the loss of destination it presupposes disrupts the way in which bodies fit their functions and destinations. What it produces is not rhetorical persuasion about what must be done. Nor is it the framing of a collective body. It is a multiplication of connections and disconnections that reframe the relation between bodies, the world they live in and the way they are 'equipped' to adapt to it. It is a multiplicity of folds and gaps in the fabric of the common experience that change the cartography of the perceptible, the thinkable and the feasible. As such it allows for new modes of political construction of common objects and new possibilities of collective enunciation. However, this political effect occurs under the condition of an original disjunction, an original effect, which is the suspension of any direct relationship between cause and effect. The aesthetic effect is initially an effect of dis-identification.'

13
Mouffe 2008, pp. 154–55.

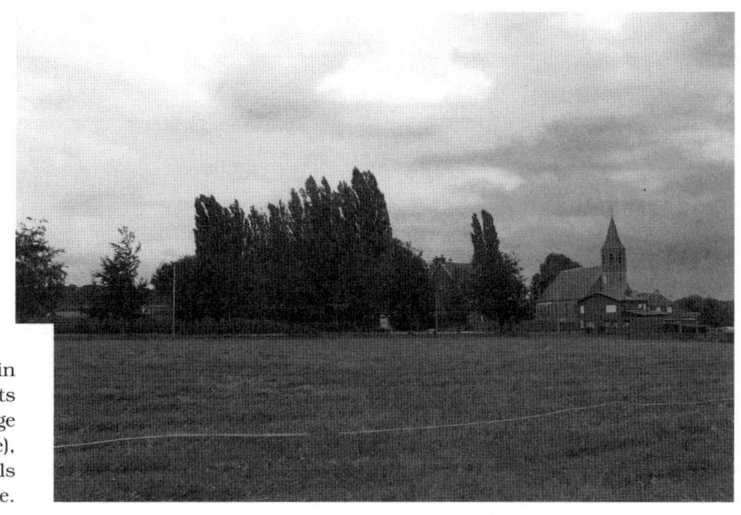

Pilootprojecten Kunst in Opdracht (Pilot Projects Commissioned Art), Village centre Ressegem (Herzele), Belgium. Photo by Niels Doncke.

rejected, but an alternative plan to make it into a special nature area could not win the support of the community either. In 2015, a special regulation from the Flemish government made it possible to start an art project that might contribute to finding a solution.[14] Now, such circumstances tend to lead to participatory projects in which the artwork consist primarily of the collaboration between the artist and the residents and the joint production generated by it. An understandable choice, as art projects that start from participation solve the problem of a practice in which art hardly plays a role and is not easily transformed in a public practice, by simply exchanging the element of 'public' by that of 'participant'. This implies a number of risks. The implicit enlightenment strategy of this approach, aimed at bringing out hidden creative forces, was already signalled by Stengers. Also, quite often what comes to the fore as the community, is only a fraction of the actual residents, and the refusal to participate is either ignored or dismissed as impotence, when it would be better to regard this attitude as a defence of the own practice. Above all, however, by emphasizing the We-experience such projects seem to be avoiding the disruptive effect of art at all costs, but in doing so they also miss the chance to let new forms of subjectivity emerge.

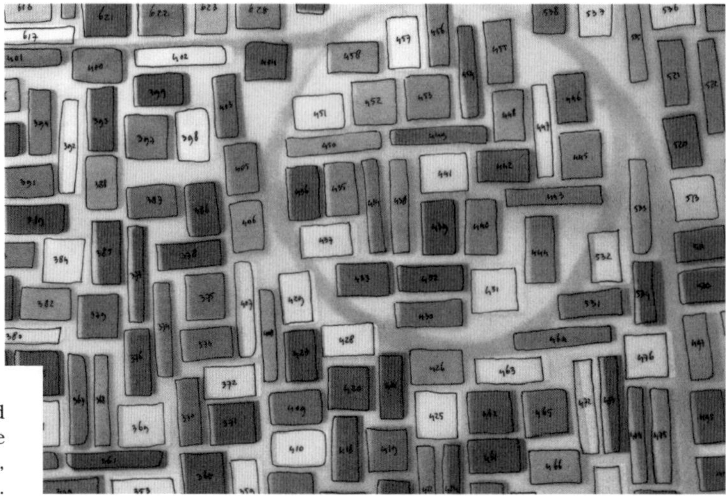

Birthe Leemeijer and David Helbich, Plan for the common meadow-land, Ressegem, Belgium.

In Ressegem two artists, Birthe Leemeijer and David Helbich, in collaboration with curator Nils van Beek, have developed a non-standard approach that meets many of the objections. They propose to divide the commons in as many lots as there are residents and let each resident manage their own tiny piece of land. By doing so the project focuses on the community as a whole, on all the residents, while at the same time testing this community's cohesion and solidarity. More importantly, in my opinion, is that this approach brings back art to the point where its authority is most evident: the subject that must decide how to relate to the impossible choices that the artwork offers. And the outcome may well be negative. Contrary to models of public outreach that are common to art institutes as well as participatory projects, in which only presence and participation count, in this project the rejection will also become visible. Those who do not participate also own a piece of land that lies fallow, thereby proclaiming what choice was made. And exactly this, this manifestation of disinterest—which questions my own faith in art in the public domain and forces me to rethink my preferences and put them in perspective—is what turns this small piece of land in Ressegem into a true public space.

It is impossible to predict what the end result of this project will be. It is up to the residents to make something of it on the basis of the 'score' provided by the artists. They chose the word 'score' aptly, as it stresses the communal framework while at the same time showing the necessity of a personal interpretation. This score does not contain an explanation or the intent of the project. It only provides the volume, rhythm and melody. This leads to a double moment of interpretation, a dual appropriation that in my view is crucial to the functioning of art and one of the great advantages of art in the public domain over art in the context of a museum. On the first level the artwork is given a place within the conceptual framework of the community. It speaks to certain problems and wishes and fits in a certain (public) practice. Without that it has no chance of succeeding. This not only applies to participatory projects, but to all art in public space. However, this alignment does not mean that the artwork fits seamlessly into this conceptual framework. On the contrary, because the second level of interpretation—on which the artwork addresses my understanding and the practices associated with that understanding—can only come about when there is something that is beyond my capacity to understand, a surplus that cannot be appropriated seamlessly. Stengers posits that practices maintain themselves by manipulating everything that they take over from other practices and not using it as it was intended. This mis-understanding is the most important manner by which art reaches groups, becomes part of practices where art usually has no place. Only in this manner does art find a new public, a public that is confirmed in its preferences and choices and at the same time is given the chance to become a different public in the future.

So here I am, face-to-face with an artwork in the public domain. Is it an artwork, or rather a concurrence of designed circumstances? Is there an intention, a meaning? There is no idea to support me. I have to find my own tentative way through this space that thereby becomes public.

ON NOT FALLING IN LINE, OR HOW TO BECOME A PUBLIC

Rogier Brom

Alone together, beyond the crowd
Above the world, we're not too proud
To cling together; we're strong
As long as we're together
—Howard Dietz

In his lyrics for the jazz standard *Alone Together*, Howard Dietz demonstrates the power of uniting. Whether it is love, opportunism, financial gains or, by contrast, a social opportunity, as soon as a group of people start to resist the will of the majority, they assume a shared identity. Whether this situation is short-lived or more permanent, the power of the group always lies in the cohesion within which each group member takes up an active position within the collective situation. A work of art can be a good reason for such a group to be formed. From the interest in the work that the onlookers share for the shorter or longer term, they form a group, which in the art world is usually called a public. And although this designation seems quite clear, what it means exactly is hard to find in the literature. In this essay I will concern myself with the question of how a group of people becomes a public. Because, whether a public is seen as fluid or as a group that can manifest itself on many different levels as well as in many time periods, there is one common element: there was a moment when it was formed. Asking questions about how an unstructured group of people makes the transition to a public brings with it a stream of other questions. I will confine myself here to the role of art objects in this.

Art is often attributed with the potential to bind groups of people. Certainly when it comes to initiatives in the area of community art or participatory art—but less directly also with much other art in public space—it is assumed that 'the public' is activated. Often it is not clear whether this public is already present or is yet to be formed. I will address the functioning of the cohesion within a group of people that can be activated and thus becomes a public, and the role that an art object has in this. The question that I ask myself is whether this role is really a bonding one or that in fact its subversive potential is much stronger. In doing so I do not use the definition of public as a place that belongs to a community nor as a series of services and objects to which a community—and not just an individual—can lay claim. I consider public to be a performative concept, a temporary community that is activated to relate itself to a whole of which it is part.

Experience as an Active Quality

Usually, when one is part of a group, one knows, to a certain extent, what the 'unwritten rules' are. The situation is clear and everyone knows the code. Even if you are not consciously aware of the code, you often have an intuitive sense of what it is. In the last edition of 2015 of *De Witte Raaf*, Rudi Laermans calls this 'experience ability' (*ervaringskunnen*), a 'potential that time and again becomes specific in relation to a particular task'. He adds that a gap that forms between the environment within which an experience originated and the characteristics of the situation in which this experience actively manifests itself, is only consciously experienced if the two are very different. Actually, Laermans states that the boundary of all practical knowledge 'coincides with the past in which it was shaped'.[1] This very awareness—and how we deal with its absence or presence—is what I intend to explore further in this essay. For example, what happens during those moments when the situation is not clear; when multiple situations and their respective codes intermingle? Can we then still speak of a gap, or is there more to it? In doing so I attempt to arrive at a definition of what public is. The suggestion I will make is that the term public in its most relevant form only applies to a group of beholders who, as a result of current circumstances, find themselves within the same network as the artwork. That these circumstances should be current, is a result of the idea that these networks only hold out as long as there is a relevant urgency.

1

Laermans 2015.

As I delved deeper into this, the Turbine Hall of Tate Modern in London was a willing subject for closer inspection. An obvious choice, as the space, besides having a museum function, also has the characteristics of a street or a square. In an article about this space and the Unilever Series in it, Wouter Davidts illustrates the dual function of this huge space with several quotations. These make clear that the space is so impressive that large groups of people come to see it. At the same time, the space remains inviting and affords the institute an opportunity to lure the newcomers into visiting the collection as well. In addition, because the floor gently slopes down from the entrance inward, one is almost literally drawn into the space and encouraged to explore it. The architectural critic Rowan Moore is quoted with his argument that the space maintains a strong public character because it is not directive in how it should be experienced. Moore considers this an important value in a time when the market is increasingly taking over public space.[2] These public characteristics are enhanced by the fact that one doesn't need to buy an admission ticket to enter the space. The scale of the hall—and how this scale is designed—is therefore one of the finds in the design that is greatly appreciated. The space partly functions as a public part of the city while still remaining part of the museum. This makes it a fine example of a place where different codes can coexist and perhaps even intermingle. One can definitely expect art in this space, but because of its public character the rules of the museum do not yet fully prevail.

During my research I chanced upon a photograph of *Up Hill, Down Hall. An Indoor Carnival*, from 2014. With this crossing of a performance and carnival celebration, curator Claire Tancons attempted to create more awareness of the potential of carnival as a medium. Tancons herself called it a 'mass public processional performance'. She admits that it is a mouthful, but it is clear that it includes a task for the visitor. When it comes down to it, Tancons wanted to make clear that this *Indoor Carnival* is not what one

2
Davidts 2007, p. 1.

would normally expect at Tate.[3] And that is perhaps an apt description of what the photograph seems to say. We see a group of performers—recognizable by their clearly different attire and attributes—standing within a circle of bystanders. This is a quite common phenomenon. When a performer is doing tricks with a football or plays an impressive drum solo on pots and pans in the Dam Square in Amsterdam, a loose circle of bystanders almost spontaneously forms around what there is to see. Everyone keeps their due distance, leaving a space that is claimed by the street performer. However, a closer look at the photograph reveals that the space in which these performers are was not formed spontaneously, in this case. A number of employees are holding a rope, delineating a place, which is probably required for the group of performers to execute their choreography properly. So the museum is actively taking on the role of guardian of the structure intended by the artist or curator or that the organization itself prefers to maintain. When we apply Laerman's term 'experience ability' here, we see that the potential of the knowledge that is present within the group has little or no possibility of becoming *specific*. Those standing behind the rope are more likely to adopt the attitude of beholder of an artwork—as

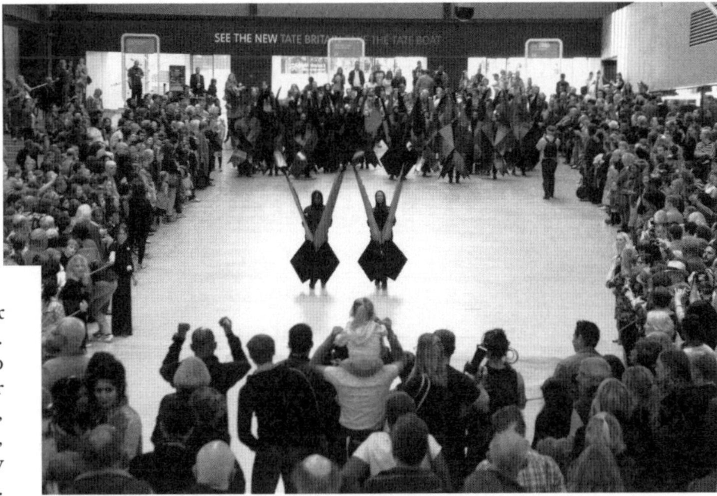

Marlon Griffith, *No Black in the Union Jack*, 2014. Part of 'BMW Tate Live: Up Hill Down Hall: An Indoor Carnival', Tate Modern, London, United Kingdom, documentation. Photo by Akiko Ota, 2014.

     ON NOT FALLING IN LINE, OR HOW TO BECOME A PUBLIC

they are used to doing in a museum—then to participate in the 'processional performance'. In other words, the specificity of the task facing those present in the Turbine Hall can hardly become manifest anymore, because of this artificial barrier. One could say that the bystanders in this case remain exactly that: bystanders, as the public that Tancons is aiming for, is simply not formed. Obviously this photograph is not a complete representation of the work, or event. Still, it does bring across much of the information one also encounters as a visitor when seeing a work or a situation for the first time. And exactly this information contains much of what can become a gap, or not. Of what, in the end, makes a group of people become a public, or not.

Lines and Collective Systems

So, my suggestion is to look at what functioning is decisive in applying the term 'public'. When does the specific community we could describe as public originate, and for how long does it exist? For me personally, the image of the floor of the school gym comes to mind. It is a somewhat simplified image but it still provides some grip on the rather abstract image of these situations. As in most school gyms, the floor of the one in my old school had a pattern consisting of numerous lines in various colours and shapes. It was a complex system that did not immediately appear logical to the untrained eye. Still, once it is explained to us, we know that different lines are used in different games. We then select only the information we need and ignore the rest. Obviously, this floor reflects a number of systems that are already present. But there was a time when all these games were played on an unmarked floor. Those who were actually playing the games decided upon the lines and rules that were required to give the game a permanent form. The lines make sure that the system can be communicated and remain active. When we apply this to the public of an artwork in public space, the moment of origination and the lifespan of the specific community arise from a complex

combination of elements. My aim is to argue that an artwork
has the potential to form a group around a shared meaning
and thus form the basis of a new line on the playing field
of public space.

Jacques Rancière provides an interesting theoretical context here. He says that a human collective consists of a node
of aspects that carry a certain degree of 'sense'. Only by a
consensus about what is meaningful, and is experienced as
such, can a collective be formed. According to Rancière, these
collectives function on three levels. The first level is an internal logic that makes a community possible; there is consensus about what is meaningful. On the second level, we
become aware of and name a dissensus that exists between
two of these communities, because this incongruity is part
of the identity of both groups. And it is this shared identity
that forms the basis for the third level. By acknowledging
that there is also a different form of community, the individuals within the *community* are made aware of their individuality. This creates the possibility to think about an
entirely new *community*. In other words: by being separate
and together at the same time, a complex relation is formed
in which the present and the future converge. According
to Rancière, the artistic proposition has the potential to
form a new community. In this sense, an artwork is 'the
people to come and it is the monument of its expectation,
the monument of its absence'.[4] It is breaking open an
entrenched logic. In a poetic sense, a new line is drawn
on the floor of the school gym. We see here the similarity
with Rancière's definition of aesthetics. He defines aesthetics as 'the system of a priori forms determining what
presents itself to sense experience'.[5] Aesthetics is at the
basis of what can be seen as meaningful, as it were.

But how do we choose what is important enough to
deserve the drawing of a new line?

In this, the artwork is a proposition, a proposal for a
choice. What moves you to make this choice and how do you
interpret the proposal? This involves more than Laerman's

[4] Rancière 2008, p. 5.

[5] Rancière 2004, p. 13,

'experience ability'. Just as with, for example, phenomenology or the ideas of Henri Bergson, Laermans seems to restrict himself to the—nonetheless quite interesting—notion that all moments that are experienced in the present are formed by experiences from the past, regardless of whether this happens consciously or unconsciously (pre-reflective). This makes each situation also multi-interpretable. But although experience and expertise determine the assessment of the situation, it is also important to look at how a possible future can be included in all this. Think for example of Derrida's idea of 'iterability'. This can be seen as the incapability of using words without determining their meaning first, which also means that the words you speak are always a copy and can as such assume a new—or in any case adapted—meaning in a new context. This new meaning is both the same as and partly different from prior meanings. Then, the words we use not only carry an existing meaning, but also the possibility of new meanings that can arise from future use in new contexts. The instability of meaning brought about by this process is sometimes compared to a game.[6]

Then how can we arrive at a more or less stable outcome? How, within a community, can there arise an internal logic that brings about a different behaviour of a heterogeneous group? And can this behaviour be influenced? In addition to the theorists already mentioned here, I would like to bring in Michael Hardt and Antonio Negri too. Their interpretation of the notion of 'multitude' is that an arbitrary group of people can bring about social effects but cannot act autonomously. This means that it is susceptible to outside influence. By contrast, the multitude supposedly is an active social subject that can act because of what the individuals within the group have in common.[7] So here we have a group that can be formed by a common denominator. In addition, this common denominator is the result of struggle, in which the seemingly opposite notions of *commonality* and *singularity* enhance each other via a communal communication.[8] So opposition to a

6 Derrida 1982, pp. 316–17.

7 Hardt and Negri 2004, p. 100.

8 Ibid., pp. 211–19.

mass reinforces the awareness of aspects of your individuality that you share with others. Naturally, communication is very important in this. A social system is formed that must be able to uphold itself. According to Niklas Luhmann, social systems, and that's what we're talking about here, are self-referential systems based on valuable communication. This communication is aimed at shaping the mutual ties between the various *events* of which the system consists.[9] The systems are maintaining themselves by reproducing their own structural parts. This would mean that the resulting collective can only be founded on parts that are already present and that are communicated internally in such a way that they remain active. With both the multitude and with Luhmann's social systems, the system only exists as long as there is relevant activity.

This activity must be allowed some room, though. Returning to the photograph of *Up Hill, Down Hall*, we may conclude that the processional propositions put forward by the works did not reach the public as such, because the museum system remained visibly and even imperatively present: the procession was treated as a work that had to be protected from the crowd around it. Those present were therefore not stimulated to relate to the work in an active manner and thereby become part of the same collective. There is no significant change in the situation or in how the environment is used, so one may wonder whether in this instance we can speak of a public for this specific work of art. By and large one could say that these people are standing there because they have come to the museum and are forced by circumstance to remain in a role in which logic dictates to keep a distance. They are not active and they will not become active as long as the museum employees guard the space with ropes. In this way it is not meaningful to go along with what the works offer.

An important argument for the relevance of activating a group of beholders of an artwork can be found in a text by Simon Sheikh. In his 'A Long Walk to the Land of the

People: Contemporary Art in the Spectre of Spectatorship'
he points out the double meaning of the English word 'audience'. 'Audience' should not be seen only as a stimulation
of participation, but should also address

> how institutions place themselves in relation to pow-
> er and use their public role to gain an audience with
> those in power, so that they may themselves, in turn,
> address power.[10]

In the case of artworks in public or semi-public space,
'power' can be described as the imperative structure that
maintains what is *sensible*, and instead of institutes it is
the artworks that can 'gain an audience with' or address
this power. One could apply Sheikh's argument to say that
the artwork has the potential to address this power structure
through the public that it activates. To underpin this I use
Giorgio Agamben's concept of 'profanation'. This means that
the power structure within a delineated field is deactivated
and the confiscated space is given back for communal
use.[11] This makes it possible to neutralize the direction
that is enforced by an imperative system in public space,
a museum context, or something in between, such as the
Turbine Hall. By placing an artwork a proposition can be
made that connects the situation to the environment or, by
contrast, creates a situation that is so different from the
environment that it has a subversive effect. Linked to Laerman's idea that a strong deviation is required to make the
users of an environment aware of a gap between the environment and the expected situation, one could say that it
is possible to change behaviour within an environment and
thereby change that environment's function as soon as this
awareness is reached. Because the system is thereby deactivated and the space is given back for communal use, which
may lead to a new system. In this case, the social system
does not reproduce itself using existing parts. It changes
course by building on meaningful differences that exist

[10] Sheikh 2015, p. 216.

[11] Agamben 2007, p. 73.

between multiple communities in order to become a new system. This situation can be regarded as a combination of the third level of functioning as ascribed to a collective by Rancière and a community in the sense of Hardt and Negri's definition of the multitude. This would mean that a public is formed at the moment that it must relate to a situation that is other than expected, while also recognizing common characteristics that can be actively shared. Although this may be a description that invites criticism, it is a workable one for mapping the potential of a work and its public. Pascal Gielen makes a similar point when he says that artists can create public space time and again. 'It is precisely in the interruption of the daily routine and of the regular social intercourse in the city that the public space originates and is charged politically.'[12] In my view, it is not so much about the space that is formed, but rather about the degree to which the users of this space manifest themselves as the cohesive group, or a public.

Public as an Active Community

In *A Grammar of the Multitude* (2004), Paolo Virno describes how characteristics of labour, politics and intellect—a trichotomy describing the human experience that goes back all the way to Aristotle—have started to mix in the post-Fordist society. According to Virno, the present-day multitude shows itself in that the so-called post-Fordist labour 'has absorbed into itself many of the typical characteristics of political action'.[13] So 'the relationship with the presence of others, the beginning of new processes, and the constitutive familiarity with contingency, the unforeseen and the possible' is not exclusive to politics. The qualifications and talents associated with politics since time memorial, are much more widely present in the multitude.[14] In the preface to Virno's text, Sylvère Lotringer writes that because of this confluence of labour, politics and intellect, they have all acquired a political dimension, because they need a public, a publicly organized space and a common language

12
Gielen 2015, p. 228.

13
Virno 2004, p. 50.

14
Ibid., p. 51.

 ON NOT FALLING IN LINE, OR HOW TO BECOME A PUBLIC

for communicating. In addition, they would all be performative 'because they find in themselves, and not in any end product, their own fulfilment'.[15] So one could say that in the gathering of the multitude lies an important breeding ground for ascribing meaning. This also shows that the potential to deal with unforeseen circumstances, complex processes and the presence of others is widely present in society. Giving back public space to *the people* through profanation has, in that sense, much greater consequences—or, if you like, a greater potential—than is perhaps often assumed.

Profanation is not just important because it neutralizes a power structure, but also because of the consequences that are linked with a new practice, according to Agamben:

'The creation of a new use is possible only by deactivating an old use, rendering it inoperative.'[16] In this Agamben sees the possibility of giving a practice back to *the people.*

In relation to the idea that deactivating a power structure within a space gives this space back to communal use, I see as a consequence that the group of people within that space is then responsible for actively looking for ways to regard the new practice as meaningful. This makes them into an active public that may continue to exist for a longer period of time. Especially in public space, visual art has a symbolic potential to stand between an old and a new practice. It is very important to realize that this change cannot be used to reach a predetermined goal. In the theory of complexity it is stated that the organization of a system (a well-known example being a school of fish) comes about as a result of the interaction between the various *constituents* of the system and its environment.[17] In this theory, one of the characteristics of the self-organizing power of complex systems is that a self-organizing process cannot be fuelled by attempts to fulfil a function, as function denotes a too limited context of only description. Fulfilling a function is therefore subject to limiting choices. Paul Cilliers then states that the self-organizing behaviour of a system

15 Ibid., p. 13.

16 Agamben 2007, p. 86.

17 Cilliers 1998, p. 89.

emerges as a characteristic of the system as a whole. The individual components only act on the basis of local information and general principles. The macroscopic behaviour therefore is a result of microscopic interactions.[18] When we look through this lens at initiatives in which art is used to bring a community closer together or make a neighbourhood more attractive, we can say that that is impossible. After all, such initiatives do not stimulate the community to actively internalize the work and give it a place in an actual relevant network. Directing such functioning does not create a public, but keeps the community at a contemplative distance.

Therefore it is crucial to be aware of the importance of choices that are made from the bottom up. If the political qualities of old are indeed widely present in society, this also increases the performative strength with regard to determining value. So far I have questioned in various ways how a group of people can choose to accept certain propositions and use these to continue as a community. I have stated that the artwork has in it the subversive potential to stimulate dissensus among various communities and thus arrive at the foundation of a new community with its public. The scale of the communities in which this happens must not be seen as too large. A single sculpture will not easily topple an entire government, but a valuable sculpture does have it in itself to reach beyond just the direct meeting between individuals and the sculpture, otherwise we would not speak of a public. In doing so it brings focus to the signs of what a smaller community sees as valuable and relevant. This brings me back, again, to the question of how choices are made in this, because the value that is assigned to an object is of great importance here. Willem Schinkel, in a response to Nathalie Heinich's new approach to the sociological discourse, says that the relevance of value is of the utmost importance. According to Schinkel, the significance of the value of an object can be seen as an outcome of social processes in which legitimate ways of positioning within a field containing more and less relatively autonomous positions create a differentiation of means of sign manipulation and thus of object creation.[19]

19 Schinkel 2000, p. 11.

Schinkel says that, initially, with artworks we cannot speak of a well-defined object at all. It is only after it has been the subject of discourse for a longer period that meaning follows, as a result of conflict. A struggle for power, power that is defined by who or what has the capacity to manipulate meaning. After all, this manipulation needs to be legitimized in order to take root and the artwork, as an object, needs this legitimization in order to function as a subversive proposition. In this I interpret power primarily as the outcome of the various complex forms of creating a community as I outlined in this essay. So not as an institutionalized power. The legitimization of choices that are made is strongly related, in my opinion, to the degree in which a public is stimulated to actively invest in the meaning of a work. Work and public depend on each other in order to arrive, on a suitable scale, at a new game that is made important enough to become fixed in the form of a community.

And so my proposition is that the value that can be assigned to an artwork in public space is to a large extent related to the possibility of an active public. I speak specifically of a work in public space, because in another context another determination of value holds true. The ideas that I have gathered in this essay seem to me, in that sense, the most relevant ones for the public space, by leaving obfuscating institutional interest aside. By forcing a gap in the experience of those present, they can be made aware of a power structure. This creates room for a proposition that neutralizes space if the public assumes an active role in the new use of this space. This is similar to what David Colander and Roland Kupers, from the perspective of the complexity theory, propose under the name 'norms policy'. By this policy 'institutions are developed to better allow people to express their collective choice about what norms and tastes should be encouraged and discouraged by society'.[20] By this they offer a possibility for structuring the presence of fluctuating norms and tastes in a society. This also means that public space can be seen as the playing field on which the collective problems of choice are being solved at a level on which communities are directed by a cohesion as would exist within a multitude. The space remains public as long as a community is stimulated to actively take part in a process that will show what norms are preferred, or: what is valuable. An artwork has the potential to maintain this process by undermining the balance that is present. Thus, public space does not create the possibility of a public, but is dependent on it. Through its flexible and subversive potential an artwork can contribute significantly to the existence of this space in which valuable communities take shape.

20
Colander and Kupers 2014,
p. 183.

DISSONANCES AND THE PUBLIC DOMAIN
An Interview with Gabriel Lester

Jeroen Boomgaard & Rogier Brom

I have been active as an autonomous artist longer than as a public space artist, but the distinction doesn't really interest me much anymore. I notice how my work only gets better the less I care about the issue. I am really a storyteller and all this weightiness of art becoming an almost religious experience is not really my cup of tea. Besides, the art world allows me to have it all my own way in an almost promiscuous manner. That is incredibly stimulating, but the art world can also make me feel claustrophobic. So, after having done an exhibition at a gallery or a biennale, I love working with architects and builders on a work in public space for a couple of months. Then that feeling of claustrophobia disappears.

Dissonance

In my view, a work of art should contain a dissonance. I usually manage to find it in my autonomous work, but in the work I make for the public space it is much more difficult because there are so many elements involved over which I have no control. When I look at the work *TWIRL* (2013) in the university library in Stockholm, I can see in how I composed it that it contains enough signature of how I treat volume and rhythm and dynamics. I always explore the limits of the space. It is really just like in music: you don't need to play false notes but you can play very close to the edge and produce dissonant notes. So in Stockholm I do see the dissonance in the work, but at the same time—and of course this changes from day to day—the question is whether I, as the maker, can find it for myself too. Quite often I don't know if I can. What I do notice is that in my autonomous work I encounter my own dissonances much sooner, as if there is more room for it. You know, I sometimes simply feel whether a piece is an applied or an autonomous work. For me, applied work is then the commissions, which involve many restrictions. There is a clear difference between the trust that a museum director or a curator puts in your project and that of some committee

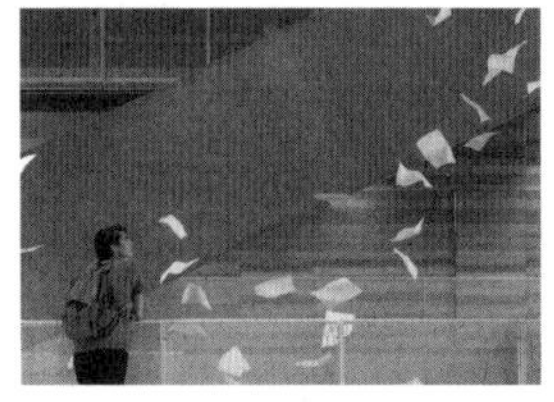

PolyLester, *TWIRL*, 2013, installation, 120 A4 papers suspended on metal wires, commissioned by Konstradet, Stockholm, Sweden.

for state art in Stockholm that makes a preselection, which is then presented to a school board. Autonomy is pushed, in the good sense of the word, by the own initiatives of an individual or institute, or a curator, for example. They say: I set you free, I launch you. With commissioned art you remain earthbound. And of course there are exhibitions for which a curator wants you to work within a certain theme, but I see that as applied work as well.

In the case of *TWIRL*, there is a bit of humour involved. It is as if someone threw the pages of his thesis into the air. It's a very nice idea that it hangs throughout the building there, timeless, but it doesn't have the same abstract complexity as some of my other works. It's not that I make easy work, it's just that I think that some work is too complex for public space. At the same time, it is fun to work in public space because you have to come up with original solutions. You are actually designing and that is a completely different ballgame. I work with a technical team. When it comes to art in exhibition spaces I am not really concerned with technical calculations but rather with research. The overall picture is quickly arrived at and as I work with a small team, it takes less coordinating. With applied work, on the other hand, you are actually invited to be a host. As a host in the public space you have to be aware of the well-being and

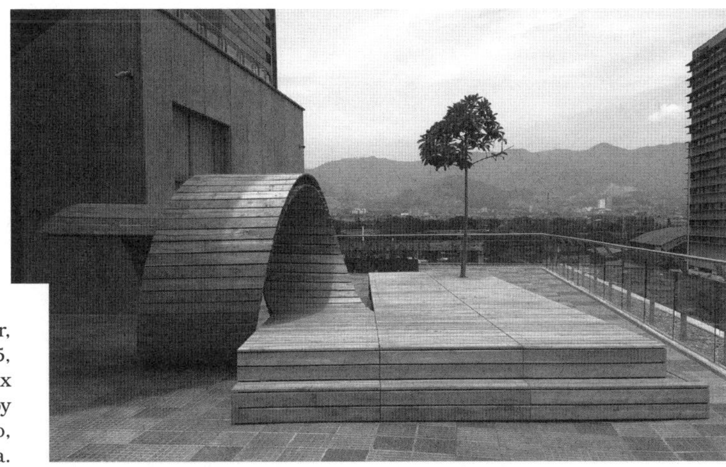

PolyLester,
Peel # 2 Twisted, 2015,
sculpture, 250 x 800 x
400 cm, commissioned by
Museo de Arte Moderno,
Medellin, Colombia.

    DISSONANCES AND THE PUBLIC DOMAIN

comfort of the people who use that space. This can make it more difficult to find a dissonance. With the *peels*, for instance, I discovered a gesture that I make. With the *peel* I peel something, so you then have a place where something was and you have the form of that which has come off. In this I recognize the things that interest me. It is sort of like frozen time, but there is also movement in it because, depending on how you see it, you experience it differently. At the same time I see that a *peel* is a nice spot to hang in or sit on. So I also see it as a sculpture you can place in a park for people to have a picnic, hang out, or climb on. This means that such a work has to be made hooligan-proof. So it can be easier for me to find my own dissonance in work that I create for an exhibition. After all, a lot of attention and focus goes into all those things you come up against in placing a work in the public space. Still, if we would look at all the projects I have done in the public space—more than 25 by now—I could point out some of them where for instance a 'skin' has grown that proved to be the breakthrough for that work. Or I suddenly notice a beautiful wood joint that really was simply needed to make it sturdy. So things do happen. Whereas in autonomous installations, I will say much easier that the work turned out exactly as I intended.

Commissioned Work

Whether your work remains autonomous also depends on how commissions are given. There is much room for improvement here. Commissioning bodies often demonstrate amateurism, lack of enthusiasm and bureaucracy. Fortunately, there is an interest in my work abroad too. I am presented with six or seven opportunities each year, and I usually seize two or three of them. Which ones I choose depends on their originality, focus on solutions, budget and whether they allow me to appeal to people. A monument to someone's memory can of course be made into a celebration, whereas someone else would focus on mourning. You can even use animals, when it is really about people. There is that liberty.

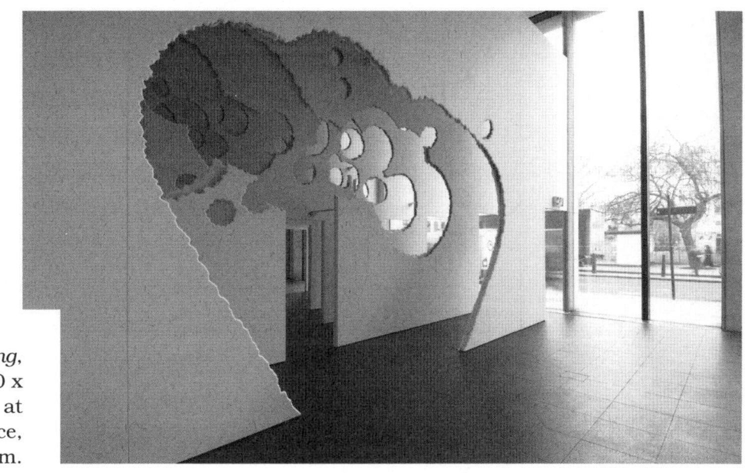

Gabriel Lester, *Big Bang*, 2007, installation, 500 x 700 x 900 cm, exhibited at Bloomberg Space, London, United Kingdom.

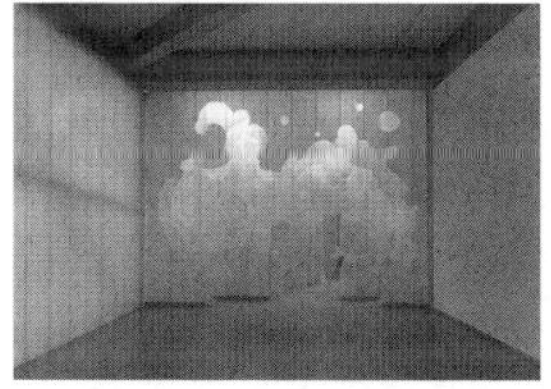

Gabriel Lester, *Big Bang Pang*, 2013, installation, 500 x 400 x 400 cm, commissioned by Sifang Museum, Nanjing, China.

All the same, I think about doing it in a way to make me proud enough to include the work in my portfolio and at the same time translate it for the people who have to sign off on it, in a way that makes them feel they are getting something that relates to why they began the process in the first place.

Especially in the new structure of PolyLester which is the frame I have created within my practice for my work in public space—in five years' time, I hope to have commissions that are better in the sense that I can also find that dissonance and autonomy in those works. Or at least can claim them fully. One of the criteria for work to be listed under PolyLester is that it lasts for more than a year. Although I have, for instance, also done a project in which I made a cut-out in a building (*Big Bang*, 2007). It was a museum piece that I conceived around the time my mother died, from the basic concept of a kind of ascension. Later I was asked to do this work again in Nanjing and since I don't often repeat my work, this was in fact almost a commission. But if you would remove the building around it and place the structure at the entrance of a park, it would still be a very good work. In this case the work therefore also comes under the heading of PolyLester, as a commissioner may be looking for an interesting entrance area.

 DISSONANCES AND THE PUBLIC DOMAIN

When I think about what I want my work to achieve in public space, it is to activate a location. This is true for most of my work. And I don't mean for the location to become interactive or invite participation. What I mean is that I install a work that is being activated by its users and the people who pass by. You can achieve this by inviting people to take place on a stage, but also by orienting the public's gaze. A well-known example of this is how National Geographic places those large yellow frames in the landscape. It is similar to the deliberate choice, in designing a house, to place a window in a certain spot. It directs your gaze for ever after. I find it wonderful to place such windows in public space.

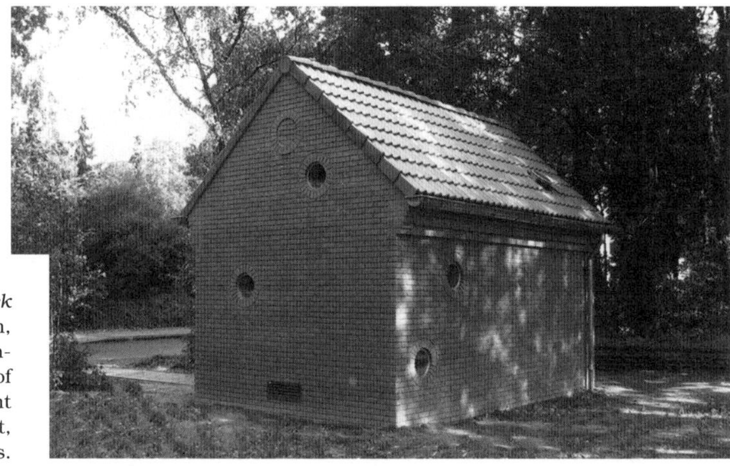

PolyLester, *Roombeek Water*, 2012, installation, 500 x 300 x 400 cm, commissioned by the City of Enschede Department of Social Development, the Netherlands.

This element of activation is perhaps strongest in my work in public space. In my twenties I wrote a lot of stories that were explicitly socially committed and were really about fate. In my films I deal with the soul, with spirituality, introspection, awareness and even with religion. It's in these films, but not really in the stories. And in my autonomous visual art I am expressly concerned with activating the imagination. Activating the human body is much less important here, whereas in public space this physical aspect becomes much more prominent. Body language is one of the elements that interest me in this. If a sculpture has a body, then what is its posture and body language? This type of questions really come from my experiences in public space.

Another important aspect of my work is the idea of the mystery. Mystery can be found in the public space too, especially by hiding something. For example, in the Roombeek quarter of the city of Enschede I made a little house that is based on these old-fashioned electricity substations with double steel doors and a small window, which is sometimes sealed. I grew up in a village that had such a substation, and it was the only small house that had no windows and on top of that it made a buzzing sound. So there was definitely mystery in that. In Roombeek I have made such a small house that is pierced by periscopes at six points. So it does have round windows, but one looks out on the woods, the other on the sky and through the next one you look at the other side of the house. This refers to the system of conducts inside such boxes. It is actually also a commission to wrap something up. So if you are asked to hide something for the public space, you can discover the mystery.

The same goes for *Transition* (2012), which I made for dOCUMENTA (13), in Kassel. In every respect, this work is exactly how I wanted it. At the dOCUMENTA I was free to create whatever I wanted. I had just had a solo exhibition in Museum Boymans Van Beuningen in Rotterdam, for which I already thought I would make the best work of my life. But I didn't quite succeed, as there were a number of things I would have liked to have done differently. Then came dOCUMENTA (13), and that was, and still is, one of the high points in my career. Also because my mother had been taking me there since I was twelve. She had studied art history and to her these exhibitions were the Olympic Games of art. My idea then was not to make the best work ever, but one that I had been wanting to make for a very long time. Even if no one would like it, I could still say that I had liked it for ten years already, so I would probably think it was good. It was a drawing

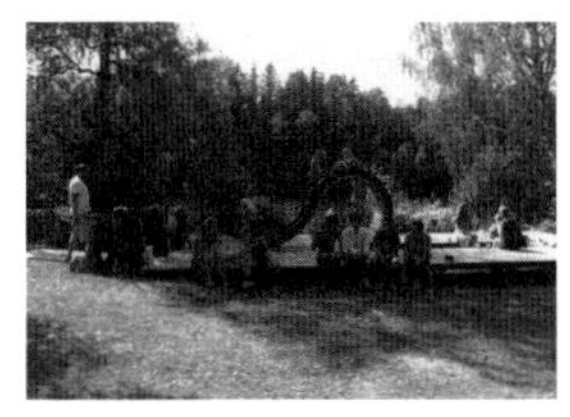

PolyLester, *Sexappeal*, 2014, sculpture, 300 x 800 x 300 cm, commissioned by Gagnef Festival, Gagnef, Sweden.

DISSONANCES AND THE PUBLIC DOMAIN

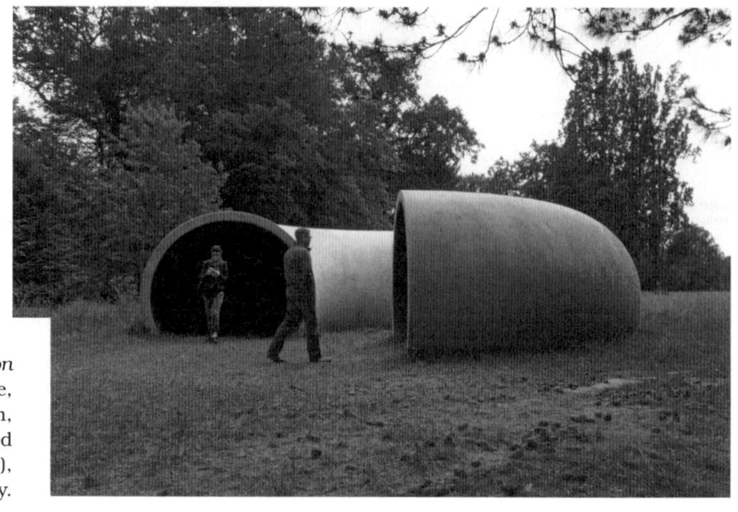

Gabriel Lester, *Transition
N34*, 2014, sculpture,
250 x1000 x 800 cm,
originally commissioned
by dOCUMENTA (13),
Germany.

from 2002, which I had already worked out quite beautifully at the time, and in 2012 I made *Transition* from it. The work has to do with my notions of narrative and cinematography. It is a movement you make from one perspective to another, a kind of cross-fade.

Of course you never know how the public will treat your work. With the *peels* I have noticed that if they make a full curl, thus providing a sense of security, I give people both a stage and the space to retreat in. That works quite well. For the exhibition in Boymans I had the idea of putting many objects on wheels. This would create a sense of coming and going in the exhibition and at the same time it was a playful reference to the Dutch policy of tolerance: visitors were not actually allowed to touch the pedestals, but it was tolerated all the same. And there was indeed a kind of flow, like in the bend of a canal were all the flotsam gathers in one place. And you learn from that. Because later we were asked to do the interior at Fort Vijfhuizen and there we introduced the same kind of flow by placing pieces of furniture and objects on wheels. We heard from visitors how much they liked that. So if one day a hotel wants me to design their lobby, I can say that I've had good experiences with this and know how to do it even better now.

I find it interesting that although *Transition* was made for an exhibition, it now stands in the Dutch province of Drenthe, somewhere along the N34. Although at dOCUMENTA it was also in public space, it was not a commission so I do count it as an autonomous work, which happened to be in the context of an exhibition. But then I was approached by

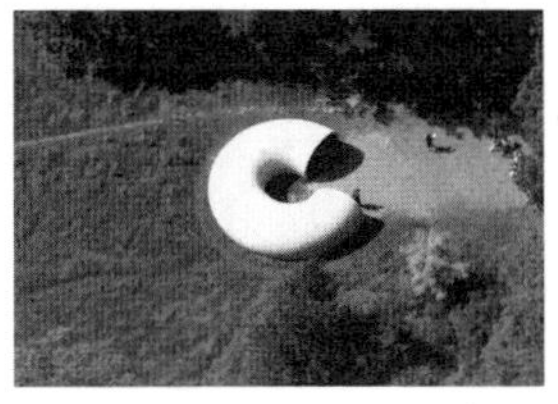

Gabriel Lester, *Transition N34*, 2014, sculpture, 250 x 1000 x 800 cm, originally commissioned by dOCUMENTA (13), Germany.

the province of Drenthe, who wanted to adopt the work, which meant it would now be in a completely different context, in public space. I grew up in the neighbouring province of Groningen, and now this work is only a stone's throw away from *Spiral Hill/Broken Circle* (1971) by Robert Smithson, so in terms of context the idea was appealing. It actually looks very good at its current location. And it definitely retains its mystery, even more so than in Kassel, precisely because it is not in an art context now. If you go inside, you find a world of traces from previous visitors, although it has on occasion been used as a public toilet.

So *Transition* worked quite well at dOCUMENTA, and it does so in Drenthe too. Perhaps it even becomes stronger as it slowly deteriorates. It is a work that I am very content with, although I am certainly not content with everything I make. This is inherent in my way of working, but it also has to do with my sense of reality. Just like there are no bands or musicians who only make good records. There are even few albums on which all tracks are good. The same goes for all filmmakers and artists. Many artists are paralysed by the idea that everything should be just right, but that is so unrealistic, and unpractical. What works for me is: try, fail, try again, fail better. I can only look at the next work, hoping that it will succeed. And artworks often change in context and even in meaning and appreciation over time. Again, like musicians, who can have very interesting periods followed by ones that are not interesting at all. Especially with commissions, I find that I am quite good in assessing what the situation requires. I am very pragmatic. Although lately I ask myself more and more whether that is really what I want in that particular situation. It's nice to have a talent for really understanding everyone in a group of twenty collaborators, but if, at the end of the day, you have the feeling that you have not been able to tell what you think that it is about, then that's not good. So that is a risk. At the same time, one should not be exclusively driven by ego. But the funny thing is that the time pressure associated with a commissioned work can sometimes prevent me from an awareness of the entire situation, which benefits the purity of the work. At other times, though, you have to show total empathy with people having their say at public meetings and it's the public that selects the work. This can make you become a pleaser. Then I put myself under pressure, because I have made a commitment, and sometimes I make choices based on what I think someone else wants, because I don't yet know what I want myself. In that regard, I think that every artist will recognize the situation when a curator makes a thematic exhibition for which he appropriates your work. That is a very awkward situation, to no longer be able to point out what you mean by your work yourself.

Of course you have to make sure to get satisfaction from somewhere. I am fortunate that there is much demand for my work and I could decide to produce half as much as I am producing now. That would give me more time to brood on projects. But as I said earlier, some projects that are created very fast are also very pure and if I brood on something for a very long time it doesn't necessarily get better. Besides, not all projects cater to the same demands. Finding original solutions in public space is just great fun to do.

Transcript: Sietske Roorda

THE BLIND SPOT
Art and Politics in the Netherlands

Steven ten Thije

Last year, the Netherlands was briefly shaken by an unprecedented polemic concerning a presupposed 'excess' of public visiting the *Late Rembrandt* exhibition at the Rijksmuseum.[1] The exhibition, which broke all records in terms of visitor numbers, had pushed the 'blockbuster' model to its end. In newspapers and social media, bitter voices bubbled up from the visiting masses stating that the crowd made viewing of the works impossible. The savvy museum director, who had undoubtable rehearsed countless scenarios on how the exhibition was going to be received, for a moment even lost his cool and grumpily told the complainers 'to buy their own Rembrandt, if they wanted private viewing'.[2] Of course, his media intelligence made him correct his mistake quickly, but when the final Late-Rembrandt had left the building, the country was left with a whole new problem to contemplate: what to do with too much public?

The event was all the more remarkable as it stood in such stark contrast with the aggressive sentiment against the arts which had held the Dutch art world captive only four years earlier and resulted in the largest cuts in the budget for culture of the post-war period. Liberal and populist politicians condemned the arts for its left-wing bias and minimal public outreach, in a harsh campaign. As prime minster Mark Rutte summarized the sentiment when asked if the proposed cuts in the culture budget weren't excessive, 'art institutions are standing with their back to the sector, holding their empty wallets towards the government. They should turn around.'[3] Did he perhaps know that while he was riding the wave that art was a 'left-wing hobby' (the frame introduced by the most notorious populist critic Geert Wilders), that probably at that very moment the preparations for the *Late Rembrandt* exhibition had started?

The two paradoxical events indicate that there is profound confusion as to where the real difficulty lies in the dynamic between art and society. The liberal,[4] populist

[1] See for instance this news article published on the site of the Amsterdam television station AT5, 'Ruim 400.000 bezoekers, maar ook honderden klachten over drukte in Rijks'.

[2] Wim Pijbes, quoted in Kooke and De Lange 2015.

[3] As quoted in Zantingh 2011.

[4] Note that in the Dutch language the notion 'liberal' has a very different meaning than in the United Kingdom or the United States. In Dutch, liberal does not so much refer to progressive, 'liberal' values, such as 'pro choice', but more to the political/ideological viewpoint that society is best served if individuals are free to do as they please. Liberal in the Netherlands therefore refers to non-government intervention and faith in the free market.

politicians argued that the arts had isolated themselves in solidly buttressed ivory towers devoid of any real public interest. However, it is hard to reconcile this image with the fact that the statistics show a steep increase in public outreach in the last decades. Even if not all arts scored equally well (experimental, contemporary art always has had more difficulty to reach a vast public than the classic arts) the overall participation of the population was not something to shed tears over. If, in the 1950s, only two and half million museum visits were recorded on a population of ten million, 2015 celebrated a new year record of 38 million visits on a population of 17 million.[5] Even if a quarter of those visits were tourists, one could still claim that enjoying the arts had become hobby number one in the lowlands.

The higher-educated part of society may be the main factor behind these numbers but that doesn't mean that only a small elite uses the art infrastructure. In the post-war years, Dutch society realized enormous jumps in welfare and wellbeing, which also had positive effects on how many people in society engaged with the arts. At the end of the twentieth century, the indigenous Dutch were better educated and enjoyed a substantially higher standard of living, from which the arts profited happily. Even if those with higher education remained the prime users of art, they no longer were a minority in the country. At 35 per cent they are a substantial group, and growing.[6] The most puzzling question therefore is how it has been possible that in one decade the largest budget cut in the arts was realized under the pretext of little public participation, while simultaneously public use of the art infrastructure had never been so high? Offering an answer to this question is the objective of this text.

The Individual at the Centre— from Thorbecke to Boekman

First of all, the source of this blindness to the actual public outreach of art dominating both government circles and

5
Wegerif 2008; for data of 2015, see Musea 2015.

6
See for instance CBS 2005.

7

On the public support for the budget cuts see Van den Dool 2011.

public opinion is not simply the result of effective demagogy.[7] It is obvious that the nationalist populist Wilders has a great talent for pushing public debates in specific directions, but still the sentiments that he manipulates have to exist in some form already for him to do this. What the statistics make clear however, is that these sentiments cannot be linked to an actual disinterest in the arts. The question therefore remains: what is the real frustration with the arts? It is difficult, if not downright impossible, to bring the exact motive of this majority to light, but there was one argument that did appear with force in parallel to the imagined lack of public: the over-dependence of the arts on public funding. On social media in particular there was a barrage of accusations branding artists as parasites hooked on public funding. Of course the combination of these two arguments produced the strongest negative emotion: spending public funds on 'unwanted' art. Yet it seems that especially the co-existence of these two sentiments somehow provides the key to resolve the mystery. Perhaps art was not so much unwanted, but rather its public value was little understood.

As if by fate, it is the then State Secretary for Culture Halbe Zijlstra, responsible for designing and implementing the notorious cuts on culture who can help us trace the origin of this paradox. During an interview in his office he was asked to tell something about the artworks in his room.[8] These works had been selected personally by Zijlstra, as is tradition in the Netherlands. Members of the cabinet can select art from the national collection for their offices. Zijlstra however had to confess that he had forgotten the name of the artist. The explanation he then gave for his remarkable memory lapse was interesting. He stated that when experiencing art he was searching for an affective response. When that emotion occurred, he was happy, regardless of who had made the work or why. The answer demonstrated a radical individualism quite at odds with his public role. Zijlstra was in charge of the public

8

Bockma 2011.

BEING PUBLIC

funding of art, yet his own experience of art seemed completely devoid of any notion of public value in art. Even the most basic ingredient of living in a community—interest in the other—was missing. The art was there for him to enjoy, full stop. Zijlstra appeared oblivious to the fact that art has existed throughout human history primarily within the framework of communal life or even as a context for political operations, as in the king's court. When looking at the historical relationship between modern Dutch government and the arts, however, it becomes clear that Zijlstra's attitude is not an anomaly, but to some degree even the norm.

The vision of the liberal Zijlstra shows strong affinity with the visions of the Dutch ur-liberal Johan Rudolph Thorbecke, who, as co-author of the Dutch constitution, was one of the principle architects of the modern Dutch state. In addition to writing the constitution Thorbecke had also formulated, more or less unintentionally, the principle that would be leading in Dutch cultural policy for more than a century. The history of what happened is by now well known. In a parliamentary debate in 1862, Thorbecke was asked why there was no mention of art in the 'Troonrede' (an annual speech delivered by the King on the occasion of the start of the Dutch parliament's session). To this he replied that 'the government is neither a judge nor an authority in affairs of arts and sciences'.[9] Later in the twentieth century this principle was reinstated as a means to defend art's autonomy, which has somewhat obscured the more ideological nature of Thorbecke's remark to which Zijlstra returned.[10] Thorbecke perhaps valued the independence of the arts, but not because art possessed a unique autonomy. As a liberal he held the view that almost everything should exist independent of the state. Thorbecke was convinced that the government should limit itself to only those tasks that would allow society to self-develop. The government's main role was security and a levelling of the playing field to allow for free competition. Every other intervention should be done

9
A detailed account of the debate is given in Boekman 1939 (1989), pp. 39–44.

10
An short overview from the impact of Thorbecke's principle on the Dutch relationship between art and government can be found in Pots 2009.

with the utmost discretion. Thorbecke thereby practiced what he preached, with great fidelity. He, for instance, was a great lover of music and was known to even schedule debates in such a manner that the members of parliament and he himself could attend good concerts. Nevertheless he made a clear distinction between what he could do as an individual and what the state should do. The government should not intervene at all, ideally, and if it were to act, it should merely support already existing private initiatives in society. Zijlstra's individualism returns to this original liberal approach to art, which recognized that art certainly had merit and could be an important source of inspiration, but for it to flourish, it was best left to the invisible hand of the market.

The affinity between the contemporary liberal Zijlstra and the Dutch liberal godfather is nothing to be surprised about. What is surprising, is that one can find certain structural elements of this view also in the opposing social democratic view. Within Dutch political history, two schools of thought in particular have run counter to the liberal view on art policy: the Roman-Catholic and the social democratic view. Especially the latter is interesting to explore somewhat more carefully as it has been the natural adversary to the liberal position in the past decades. Together, the liberal and social democratic view have spanned the bandwidth of the Dutch political landscape for quite some time, these last four years even in a coalition government. The social democratic view therefore has existed as the main opponent to the liberal view. How then did the social democrats conceive the public role of art? The key figure on the social democratic side to consider is Emanuel Boekman, who published a well-researched study on the relationship between the government and art in 1939.[11] His views show a great difference with the liberal position, yet at certain vital points he almost invisibly aligns with them.

Boekman indicates in the opening of his study that he

11
Boekman 1939 (1989).

BEING PUBLIC

does not intend to give a substantial reading of the relationship between art and state as such, but wants to focus on the existing relationships between government and art in the Netherlands.[12] The core of the study does not focus on social democracy per se, but gives an overview of the different political schools of thought that have been leading in the debate on art and government in the nineteenth century. After this the study deals with all the different fields where the government engages with the arts: monuments, fine arts, museums, music, et cetera. What makes the study even more than a mere description is that Boekman at no point is reluctant to offer his own opinion. His general sentiment thereby is a strong and persistent critique on the lack of government interest in the arts. Still, the social democratic part of this critique remains more or less hidden, but after more than 170 pages of critical assessment of the Dutch engagement with the arts, he ignores the limit he has set himself and makes some more general statements on how the government should fund art that are linked to the social democratic view.

When asking himself the question how then the government should 'support' the arts, he answers by stating that one should not confuse support for the arts with support for artists. The latter refers to the interests of a group and this is not the focus of art politics. This group, according to the social democratic vision, should be socially protected as any other group, but this is not the goal of the government's specific engagement with the arts. 'The artist', as he states not long after this,

only has value within and for the community through his work, which he gives it. It is in this work that the government can stimulate him, if the work deserves this, by either commissioning or buying it.'[13]

What specific values he refers to in the case of art becomes somewhat clear in the pages that follow.

12
Ibid., p. 5.

13
Ibid., p. 185.

The first relevant observation he makes concerning the value of art is that in a state, in which citizens carry an individual responsibility, it is a characteristic of art that it develops according to its own laws. In this development one will also notice the impact of social and political relationships and views, but to impose such views would mean a misrecognition of the essence of art and would show a paternalistic attitude, which would be disadvantageous for the arts.[14]

Here Boekman commits himself to art as an autonomous domain. Art has links to society, but these links can only be fostered by focusing on the art itself. He then uses this statement to argue for special advisory committees of artists or experts to advise the government in decisions pertaining to the arts.

Boekman then continues by stating that next to commissioning and acquiring high quality artistic production, the other major role of the state is to stimulate the interest in art.[15] This second major task for the government is more explicitly social democratic. In the liberal nineteenth century, Boekman observes, the engagement of the government with the arts mostly benefited the elite community of bourgeois citizens who were already in a position to enjoy the arts. In the early twentieth century, when the recent social emancipation of the wider population began, the government has to widen its outlook. 'Interest in art, or as sensitivity for culture', he states

cannot exists with the masses, if welfare is low, if education is insufficient, if working days are too long, and living conditions are poor. However, when all this improves, the spiritual level is also elevated, and the need for values that lie beyond the struggle for everyday survival.[16]

14 Ibid., p. 186.

15 Ibid., p. 187.

16 Ibid.

Boekman here closely links the value of art to the individual emancipation and growth of man. When the most basic needs are fulfilled the individual starts to develop an interest in art, and this new, more sophisticated need should also be attended to by the government. In what follows, this link between the development of the individual and the value of art, keeps returning. Boekman, for instance, states that art education allows the student to learn 'to enjoy beauty', which he considers part of 'the full life' and 'an essential part of our being'.[17]

17 Ibid., p. 193.

Art, Society and Transformation— the Invisibility of Politics

What is absent from Boekman's view, is the notion that art can actively contribute to the transformation of society. He considers art a basic anthropological quality of the human subject but not explicitly linked to life in a community. This becomes especially clear when he discusses the challenges that museums face in modern times. First, he states that the 'beauty and joy that art can give are not fixed givens'. It is a statement that would make it easy for him to then introduce the relativity of art to historical progress and link art explicitly to society. However, Boekman takes a different route and continues by writing: 'The beauty, of course, remains the same, however, the receptivity for her works changes over time.'[18] Instead of seeing art as influencing change in society, he considers it the role of museums to make sure that at each point in the development of society, the stable quality of beauty, can be enjoyed by all.

18 Ibid., p. 202.

Art is considered part of the 'full life' and is important for people to develop their entire being, yet this has no direct relationship to questions of politics or government. Where Boekman and Thorbecke differ is that Boekman feels the government should actively intervene to allow each person to share in the joys of the full life and he is not convinced that the private initiative will be sufficient to create a good artistic climate. Boekman wants the government to take an active role in protecting heritage, furthering artistic production through commissions, and introducing all of society to the value of good art in the form of decent and beautiful housing, next to accessible public art institution and general art education. Where the views of these two men align is that both feel that the involvement of the government should be done discretely and that the active involvement of the government introduces the risk of drawing art into the political sphere. They share the view that the government, in the case of art, to some degree is a necessary evil, which in an ideal world would disappear. Theoretically, for Boekman, if all of society would be equally well educated in the enjoyment of beauty and they would spend their means without the steering hand of the government on art, government intervention would no longer be necessary. The idea, in other words, that art in some sense is inherently public in the sense that art participates in the most public activity of all—politics—is not entertained by either Thorbecke or Boekman.

Even in the decades following the Second World War, in which the social democratic labour party was a big political force in the Netherlands and during which even real Marxist thinking took root in Dutch society and its art community, art's position outside of public life and politics was in a subtle way maintained. On the surface, Boekman's paternalistic desire to elevate the uneducated masses was broken up and steps were taken to link art directly to social processes. Especially one policy paper 'Discussienota Kunstbeleid' (Discussion Paper Art Policy), published in 1972, in many ways broke with the individualism that could be found with Boekman implicitly and with Thorbecke explicitly.[19] The paper repositioned art policy within the field of welfare policy and stated that the government should support especially those moments where art engaged with society. This paper identified that art has a 'forming' function as an expression of the fact that our total behaviour, both individually and collectively, our complete cultivated surrounding,

19 Ministry of CRM 1972.

is subject to design.' Next to this, the writers identify a 'social function' of art, which refers 'to art's capability to bring people closer to one another, while keeping their own identity. In this instance art is a means to live together.'[20] Beyond the domain of the individual this policy paper builds on the idea that art has a distinct and special relationship with society, whereby the government's involvement with the art should focus on those places where the two meet.[21]

Here an explicit understanding of art as having a role in the public sphere is taken up, only in the end the relationship with the government remains complicated and blurred. When defining the 'position of the policy', the authors of the paper state:

> The policy position of the government in relation to art within its policy terrain has to be seen on the one hand from the perspective of a historical, cultural political background, on the other as following the line that is set out above (that the government stimulates special [social] functions of art). This means that the government to some degree lets art be art. The government observes the functioning of art, acts on the basis of this observing attitude, and follows attentively the autonomous development of art and society.[22]

This section is meant foremost to explain that within the bureaucratic methodology that will be used to deploy the ideas outlined in the paper, the government will, as it did before, refer to expert advice from the field and will keep a 'distance' from the process of selecting what specific artistic initiatives to fund. This more technical strategy, however, does have the effect that it leaves one important aspect within the social function of art undiscussed: the real relation between art, politics and government.

The general blind spot in the discussions on the relationship between art and society is the inability to understand

20
Ibid., p. 18.

21
Ibid., p. 30.

22
Ibid., p. 40–41.

if and how art's social function relates to politics. The fact that the policy paper, for example, is the result of a political process in which differing or even opposing positions have wrestled with each other and have brought forward this position, is not explicitly regarded as something to which the arts actively contribute. The dichotomy that pervades the Dutch discourse on art and society is that there is a relationship, but the political practice that forms the centre of life in a community is placed in a separate domain. When the policy paper is analysed structurally, we see that Boekman's strategy of building on the merit of art for the individual is extrapolated to society as a subject. The fact that society is made up of individuals who differ and oppose each other—differences that are negotiated through political processes—is not linked to the specific contribution art can make. In this policy paper, art is a general 'need' of society, but the government and the practice of politics exist separately from this need. The government is willing to support this need, but as it is afraid that its own involvement will somehow disrupt the organic functioning of art in society, it tries to keep a safe distance.

There is, of course, one evident explanation for this reluctance to link art to politics in the 1970s, as the most recent and even then still current examples of regimes that brought art explicitly into the political domain—Nazi Germany and the Soviet Union—were very problematic. Still the consequences of refusing to make explicit the manner in which art belonged to public life and how as a result it then would also link to politics, came at quite a high price. Art remained primarily a private, individual affair, with a problematic normative twist to it. Art was considered a merit to the individual, but not all art was considered beneficial to the same degree. Willingly or not, this approach turns art into a normative and elitist enterprise, even if, as is happening today, a vast majority of society engages with art. It is evident that not all art can be funded and choices need to be made. However, if there is no other way to assess what art is of more merit to the functioning of society and its inherent political process, then the only criterion left is quality. This turns the art professionals entrusted with the task of selecting into paternalistic guardians of artistic quality. In this situation, raising the level of education in society even backfires in a strange manner, as it becomes less and less understandable to an educated community why a group of experts should decide which art is good and which is not. When the paternalistic attitude becomes more and more problematic, it becomes increasingly difficult to defend judgements of quality if they cannot be linked to the main objective of public funding, namely to benefit the community as a whole, in all its diversity.

'Render visible what had not been'— Rancière on Art and Politics

This might explain the core problem of Dutch art policy, but it does not answer what type of policy would work. Providing such an answer is far from simple as it requires one to answer the complex question of how art participates in public life, in politics? It is clear that in a democratic society, such as the Netherlands, the link of art to politics cannot be based on certain political positions. In other words, art is not political because, for instance, it represents the views of one party or the other. Some artworks may make explicit political statements, as Picasso's *Guernica* does as a critique of fascism, but still art's contribution to politics does not lie in these statements. Art is more than a statement and the difficult questions is: how does the specificity of art relate to the political process?

This question has received more attention in recent years.[23] I would here like to present the views of the French philosopher Jacques Rancière, a very esteemed voice in this debate. In his text 'Aesthetics as Politics' Rancière offers a quite clear description of the relationship or, rather, interdependence of art and politics, by first analysing politics as such. 'Politics', he writes

23
Recent publications on the subject are for instance: Rebentisch 2012 and Zuidervaart 2011. The text I will refer to Rancière 2009b.

is not the exercise of, or struggle for, power. It is the configuration of a specific space, the framing of a particular sphere of experience, of objects posited as common and as pertaining to a common decision, of subjects recognized as capable of designating these objects and putting forward arguments about them.[24]

24 Rancière 2009b, p. 24.

Rancière hereby broadens the political process by letting it incorporate not merely the point of decision and the execution of power. He makes explicit that before these decisions can be made, a world needs to be created, a space defined, in which the decisions make sense. Politics is much more the formation of this space than it is the moment when one acts in coherence with the lay-out of this common space. What for Rancière is then the most relevant question is how this space is formed, and how it can change. He then turns to Aristotle in order to formulate an answer. 'Man', Rancière quotes Aristotle,

is political because he possesses speech, a capacity to place the just and the unjust in common, whereas all the animal has is a voice to signal pleasure and pain.[25]

25 Ibid.

Rancière then continues and observes that within the hierarchical world view of Artistotle it was always clear which members of society were attributed the capacity to speak (tax paying men), and what groups were considered as only having a voice (slaves, artisans, women, children, et cetera). According to Rancière, politics takes place at those moments when subjects who are considered to only have a voice, mobilize and 'demonstrate that their mouths really do emit speech capable of making pronouncements on the common which cannot be reduced to voices signalling pain'.[26] When the group stays homogenous and the understanding of the common sphere remains intact, decisions by governing bodies can be understood as

26 Ibid.

management. This management, however, turns political when the people entitled with the power to make decisions, start to take into account a different configuration of this common space. For this to happen it is vital that those subjects who were not heard before can 'render visible what had not been'. Art intervenes at this precise point, as it is able to introduce new sensations into the common sphere, which then require interpretation and can allow for a 're-distribution of the sensible', as Rancière would call it, which can be understood as the reconfiguration of what is important and what is not, what kind of practice is just and what is not. This is the real function of politics: it asks for a specific effort by the members of a political community, and therefore also requires its own 'organization' as a constructive component of a society.

In Dutch history, precisely this awareness that art partakes in politics is not theorized and therefore not accounted for within policy making and this will be one of the major challenges to face in the years to come. The discussion paper from 1972 did make a small opening to map the complex yet important relationship between art and politics, but the door that was slightly opened was quickly closed again. The 1980s saw, in a sense, a 'call to order', whereby the social component that was identified was exchanged for a more traditional focus on artistic quality again.[27] Today, this old-fashioned approach still persists. It is for instance clearly present in a small pamphlet published in 2013 by a former senior civil servant in the Ministry of Education, Culture and Science, Thije Adams. Seeking to defend the public funding of the arts, he advocates an only lightly touched-up version of Thorbecke's positions.[28] To allow the public appreciation for art to 'return' or at least 'increase', the public needs to be given a bigger role within the process of allocating funding. Adams focuses primarily on the dynamic between the serious amateur and the professional arts, who in his view hold the key to a good climate for (high) art. Again the proposed strategy is one of

[27] For an account of the general development of Dutch art politics, see Pots 2002, pp. 291–308 and pp. 323–47.

[28] Adams 2013.

retreat, but now not just of the government, but also of the layer of professional artists and critics who occupied the gatekeeper position of advisor to the government. Adams believes that including the public itself in the process of deciding what to support, combined with fostering the private initiative, are the only ways to make the public accept public funding for the arts. It demonstrates in a clear way the subtle manner in which the public value of art is misunderstood in the Dutch debate on art policy. Art here is considered public if it is appreciated by a large section of the public, yet it does not address how a group of individuals becomes 'a public', or together forms a public domain. Following Rancière, art contributes to public life, not because it is enjoyed by the many, but because it helps a community to come to terms with complicated conflicts and differences that exist within it. If the question of support for art continues to be waged as a debate on the popularity of art, then art will remain trapped in ever different forms of exclusivity, be they the elitism of experts, the elitism of the higher educated or that of the affluent, et cetera.

In 2011, this blindness has shown its destructive consequences. The Dutch community had obscured to itself the relationship between art, society and politics for more than a century. As a result, even if there is a vague understanding of art as important to society, this importance is constantly individualized. This makes it hard to truly understand the public value of art (and accept that as a result it can and even should be supported with public means as well). Art to the Dutch is either something of personal taste, or it is the taste of the specific group (ethnic, socio-economic, interest, et cetera) to which one belongs. Therefore, the general sentiment is that either the individual or the specific group should supply the means for the production of this art. This also makes it possible for people to joyfully make use of the public infrastructure for arts, while at the same time failing to understand why this is publicly funded, aside of the vague notion that art is somehow 'good'.

Today, this blindness is becoming chronic. New digital forms of communication, combined with economic and geopolitical crises, are pushing the democratic culture of the Netherlands to its limits. From a serious but respectful struggle, the political process is turning into an embittered battle, which sometimes even leads to real physical violence. When the Dutch political community remains blind to the aesthetic component of the political process, it will miss one of the key instruments it has to negotiate the conflicting views that now make up the political landscape. What, however, may still offer some hope in these difficult times, is that the starting point for making a change today is not bad. Regardless of why and how, the Dutch have created a society that is happily using its public infrastructure for art and culture (38 million museum visits last year, more than half a million visits to one exhibition) as they also have the education to do so. In other words, the Dutch are in some sense already acting in a manner that is coherent with the idea that art participates in the political process, only it is not made explicit. With relatively small adjustments, the contribution of art to society, including its political process, can increase substantially.

The main focus of these adjustments should be to identify those points where art resonates within the political process and to seek to create an awareness and a support for these moments of interlinking between art and politics. This does not mean that all support for art should be dedicated to these moments of exchange, because these moments in principle cannot be planned nor should they be. What Rancière's analysis makes explicit is that it is not so much the content of the artwork that makes a work political or not, but that a political process contains an aesthetic element of experience that is linked to artistic production. Artworks in a very literal sense allow subjects to broaden the bandwidth of what they can experience and as a result can become more aware of 'cries of pain' that are actually 'acts of speech', to use Rancière's terms. Artworks therefore don't have to be political in content in order to contribute to the political process. What art policy could support better, is the education of people so that they can realize that within the locus of their own experience already lies the seed of political action. In addition, offering more support to facilitate people to constructively insert their aesthetic experiences into public debates, through more attention on the reception of art, could also be constructive. If this can help to create an ecology in which art and the enjoyment of art can be understood as contributing to the quality of the political process, then the Dutch could reap the harvest of the garden they have somewhat unknowingly cultivated.

ART AS ENCOUNTER

Anke Coumans

A number of artists today set out to create no
more artworks. Instead they want to get out of the
museum, and provoke modifications of the space of
everyday life, giving rise to new forms of relations.
—Jacques Rancière[1]

1
Rancière 2008.

The Courage to Act

In December 2015, SIGN, a project space for young, experimental interdisciplinary art in Groningen, hosted a series of presentations concerning the projects that were being developed in the context of the Parrhesia programme. Parrhesia is part of the Being Political research lab of the research group Image in Context of Academie Minerva in Groningen. The invited artists and designers[2] had been challenged to connect the parrhesiast's brave position to their own work in day-long debate sessions a few months earlier. In his last lecture series (1983–1984) the philosopher Michel Foucault (1926–1984) worked with this Greek concept, which directly opposes the notion of rhetoric. Where the rhetoric speaker strategically aims to win the public over, the parrhesiast always speaks the unconvenient truth, regardless of the public's reaction.

2
Participating artists and designers were Woodstone Kugelblitz, Yuri Veerman, Katja Verheul, DesignArbeid, Roel Roscam Abbing, SulSolSal, Gijs de Heij en Eleni Kamma.

A group of students and alumni[3] presented the installation *The Wheel of Fortune*, in which they asked several people in the audience to join them and answer a series of confrontational questions in complete honesty (one question was, for example, what the boundaries are between art and life). In other words, they asked the audience to have the courage to tell the truth arising from the concept of parrhesia. To underline that the conversation was not meant to consist of small talk but was rather a ritual deliberately placed in the artistic space, two of them were dressed as businessmen and two others wore robes that alluded to Greek antiquity. According to the participating students the business suits referred to the financial transactions that surround spiritual practices. The artists in robes invited the members of the audience to a tent to

3
Bernardo Zanotta, Anna Ehmen, Anna Rijkens, Nia Konstantinova.

give them a hand massage.[4] In order to get the spectators to drop their passive role and to challenge them to express the bond that had developed between artists and spectators, the students asked the participants for a reciprocating act, in the form of honest answers, in exchange for the services rendered.[5]

In this essay I will discuss the specific nature of this type of art practices. In these practices the artists and their publics are moving away from the more traditional relationship in which artists merely display their art in museums or public spaces. They consist of intimate and personal processes made possible by the grace of the artistic space that is separating itself from the coded space around it. In these practices the public takes on a different role than that of the passive spectator. The involvement of the public in what art is and can be becomes part of the experience. This turns art into something to be a part of rather than something that is simply handed over to you. More specifically, these art practices allow for a time and site specific situated form of co-ownership, through which the artistic environment created by the artist becomes the condition for experiencing new ideas and insights. In relation to theatre, the French philosopher Jacques Rancière (1940–) writes in *The Emancipated Spectator* (2015) about 'theatre without spectators, where those in attendance learn from as opposed to being seduced by images; where they become active participants as opposed to passive voyeurs'.[6] These practices are not new. New is perhaps the shift of focus from public participation in processes of interaction towards developing a theatrical space that not only makes other types of expression possible, but also takes on other roles and with that, other perspectives. This notion will therefore be the main focus of this text. Whereas Jacques Rancière talks about the aesthetic space (Rancière 2004) because of its emphasis on the distribution of the sensible (*le partage du sensible*), in the case of situated art I'd rather

4
Nia Konstantinova explained: 'The very spiritual happened when we realized that these people are stepping out of their comfort zone and it was up to us to create another one which gives them space to both think on the previous conversation but also relax and connect with us. The whole scenery was lit by a light, meant for art therapy which connected our spiritual moment to the machines that we surround ourselves with and the artificial places for sanctuary that are so common today (churches, temples, graves are also artificial sanctuaries).' (Source: email exchange)

5
In Nia Konstantinova's words: 'We wanted to provoke the dislocation of the spectator from his passive and inoperative role, which is usually what happens, and be able to create a certain affinity that existed only in that moment in between us and the people who participated.' (Source: email exchange)

6
Rancière 2009c, p. 4.

speak of the theatrical or artistic space, indicating a space that corresponds to the domain of the arts. But one can also speak of a staged space, a space that has been constructed and is thus able to separate itself from the space around it. In any case, it is important that this space not only mobilizes the senses but also *the will to act*. The art students and alumni resort to the dramatization of the space for a reason. It is done in order to turn spectators into participants who are willing to act, or better yet, have the courage to act, because as Hannah Arendt (1906–1975) stressed in *The Human Condition* (1958), not only is performing an act the most human activity but also the most uncertain. In performing an act man sets something in motion that he does not completely control. Before it was made clear that *The Wheel of Fortune* was to become a truth-telling experience the students asked the visitors to take on a position within the theatrical setting they had created. This required a certain kind of seduction. In this sense, the students understood that situated art projects are founded in the spectator's courage to act.

What is essential in situated art practices is what is taking place on site. Art only becomes a situated practice when the audience enters the space and participates. Of course, it could be said that this notion differs only slightly from traditionally exhibited art and that a piece of art put on display only comes into being when beheld and given meaning by the spectator. The difference therefore concerns only the physical presence of the artist and thus the shift from watching to acting and participating. Yet the difference between the call from a passively displayed piece of art, which is easily dismissed, and the call from a physically present artist who takes you through a process you cannot escape from halfway through, is undeniable. In situated art practices there is a clear sense of a greater degree of interdependence between artist and participant. Because of the request that is made of the acting spectator there is the need for a relatively protected intimacy, a secure publicness in which only the eyes of the other participants and bystanders are present.

The Fierce Light of the Public Media

In the struggle between exhibition art that requires no action and creates spectators, and situated art practices that create a different space in which participants are encouraged to act, the public media take up different positions as reactants. The presentation of exhibition art in museums or public areas is usually accompanied by strongly influencing media coverage. Let it be clear that no one enters an artistically coded space as a blank page without any expectations, same as with stepping into a space where a situated art practice is taking place. No one was surprised or shocked to be asked by artists to become involved in an art practice in SIGN gallery. The media coverage, however, largely created and programmed the expectations of the future public. The reports not only brought the exhibition to the attention of the reader, but also affected the way the specific works were experienced, which is in turn part of the idea constructed by the same media about what art should be. This does not mean that quality cannot come across and be experienced by those affected, but it does mean that spontaneous occurrences in the encounter between art and audience are less likely to happen, and might even disappear when we let ourselves be guided by the media and that which it shines its very decisive light on. Tino Sehgal, an artist operating in the Stedelijk Museum in 2015, seems to be well aware of this. He confirms the influence of the media by prohibiting the museum to advertise for his projects. In his journal on the website of the museum, art lawyer Aernoud Bourdrez explains Sehgal's defiance as a refusal to let the world of systems enter the world in which we live. Sehgal rejected

advertising which, with the use of innovative laws in the marketing world, could have created high expectations and lured me inside. I saw no catalogue, with

> which I could have placed Sehgal's work in a museum context. I have no commercial connotation because the prices are not discussed. There are no explanatory labels in the hall that can tell me what collection the work belongs to and by which I could place the work within the context of the art world.[7]

7
Boudrez 2015.

The result is that the unprepared spectator is more or less taken by surprise by Sehgal's performances and that, besides the knowledge that the already educated observer has of performance art, only that single performance can be of reference to others. The performances were not signified in advance. Martijn van Nieuwenhuyzen, curator of the exhibition:

> His work only exists during the moment the visitor enters the museum space and must relate to one of his 'situations'. That is when it happens. Once you leave the room it is gone. It is a totally unique and individual experience at a very specific moment.[8]

8
Boudrez 2015.

In our mediatized society the light of the public—a notion Hannah Arendt explains in *The Human Condition*—has become the fierce light of the media. 'That which is public' no longer means to exist in public in the eyes of the other but to become visible in the eyes of the media. Situated art attempts to dim the media's light in favour of the view of the other.

The existence of situated art practices is crucial in light of creating a different artistic environment that is located primarily outside of the media. The examples described here provide the context of a museum or gallery in which a shift from looking to acting and from giving meaning to participating is taking place. In the next part of this essay I want to discuss how these practices become artistic spaces in themselves that influence the social spaces around them. The space that has been coded by the arts provides an even sharper contrast to the socially coded spaces surrounding it. This results in the involvement of people who do not directly belong to the inner-circle audiences of the arts within different local contexts. Because they become part of an artistic process they get to experience, perhaps for the first time, what art truly is. I would like to describe this as a different time-space that embeds itself within the space of normal, everyday occurrences, and in those spaces makes other forms of experiencing, other perspectives of meaning, and other perspectives of action possible. Not the physical creation of art but the development of an environment in which art can come into being in other ways and in new relationships with the public is inherent to the type of projects described here.

Productive Interaction with the Common Public Space

In the example of the Parrhesia project there is, as stated before, already an art environment (the gallery) within which the group develops its own space. The same can be seen in Tino Sehgal's projects in the Stedelijk Museum. He also created his own space within the museum in which a form of interaction with the public could take place other than the passive interaction between the spectator and beheld artwork.

In many other situated art projects the artistic space is being positioned within public areas of social interaction. This creates a form of synergy between the two differently charged areas. Whereas Nicolas Bourriaud placed emphasis on the origination of the social space as an artistic space and on how the social space invades the artistic space, in his influential work *Esthétique relationelle* (*Relational Aesthetics*)[9] in 1998, I want to examine how the artistic space arises from within the social space and also the interaction between these two domains. Or, in other words, where in the relational aesthetics the social space becomes an artistic space, this essay investigates the interaction between the

9
Bourriaud 2002.

two domains and the interplay through the implantation of the one space within the other. They question each other. The interaction affects both the autonomous area of the arts, the place where art only relates to itself, and the heteronomous spaces in which non-artistic, social processes take place. Some examples may serve to illustrate the interactions between the ordinary world and art that are transforming art because of how the ordinary world is entering it. The ordinary world is undergoing a similar change as art is in turn implanting itself in it.

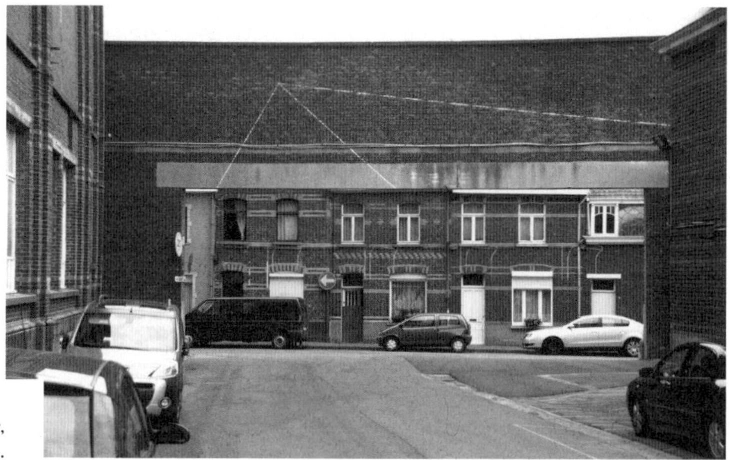

Bart Lodewijks, *Ronse*, Belgium, 2011.

Commissioned by several arts organizations and municipalities, artist Bart Lodewijks has been exploring neighbourhoods and districts throughout the world for many years. By applying chalk he transforms the neighbourhood into a temporary artwork—the influence of the artistic space on the public space. Yet his works can only 'become' if the neighbourhood is willing to cooperate. The residents must give their permission to let the artist draw on their homes. And so he draws his way from the centre spot of the football field, and on through the street, on terraced houses, Art Deco houses, and the side of a Moroccan teahouse. Finally, he manages to have his aesthetic domain enter the homes of the people. He wrote about the process in his essay *Heimwee*

10
Lodewijks, 2014, p. 119.

naar krijt ('Homesick for chalk'): 'A line is the shortest connection between two points, similar to a footstep. On foot you can get almost anywhere. I've been trying to get everywhere by drawing'.[10] However, the influence of the social space on the space of art goes beyond giving consent. That is to say, an essential part of Lodewijks' art practice is his conversation with the local residents. As they become part of his work, he becomes part of their community through listening to their stories. He comes to the neighbourhood with chalk and leaves it with stories.

This project is somewhat similar to *Academy of the People*, a project created by artist Jonas Staal and students from Academy Minerva, in 2013. In this project, an artistic strategy of art exchange was developed. This strategy consisted of the students reaching out to what were to them foreign organizations or institutions, and propose a form of art exchange to them. These organizations and institutions included the police station, Ikea, a synagogue, and an IT company. Students brought a context-specific work of art into the chosen institutions, and in turn the partner organization temporarily placed an artwork in the Groninger Museum. The proposed exchange was attractive to the partner organizations because they could now temporarily place something within the temple of art. In turn, they let students create contextualized art and place it within the organization. While the artworks that the organizations chose for the museum were fairly obvious paintings, the students wanted to make visible what was art to them in relation to the organizations. One student made an installation at the police station of all the belongings that were stolen from him in the past. Furthermore, he asked for the ritual punishment of spending one night in a cell. Another student put statues he made in the Ikea with a price tag. Because Ikea did not want to collaborate, he put Ikea's best-selling 'painting' in the Groninger Museum: the rose. A third student created an artwork in the synagogue that consisted of several holy books referring to one another. The most radical work was that of a student who chose to convert to Islam after a couple of conversations with believers as a means to enter the time-space of Islam as an artist. From then on any work she would create could automatically be placed within that context. Through these interventions in non-artistic spaces, the students used situated art to directly include people who normally might not go to the museum in what art could be: another view on a supposedly self-evident practice. The project was concluded with a series of conversations about each other's understanding of art at the Groninger Museum. The contextual art the students had made was part of an artistic exchange, a reciprocal action. The artists made the organizations part of a broader artistic discourse that both contextual art and exhibition art were a part of.

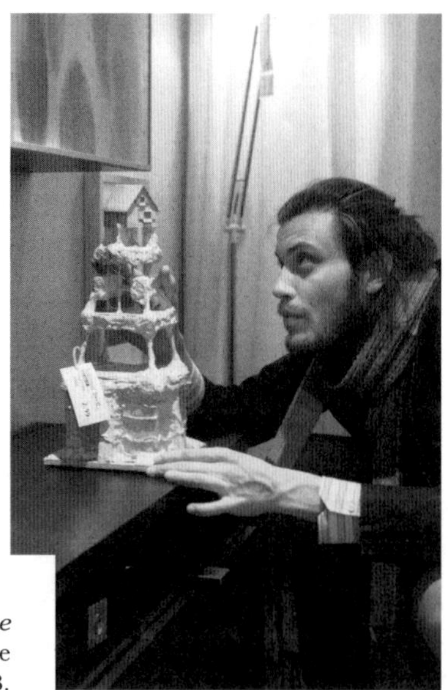

Jimi Kleinbruinink, *Statue for Ikea*, Groningen, the Netherlands, 2013.

Redefining the Art Process

In the third example, something else occurred besides the interaction between the artist and the social context: the artist redefined his or her practice of being an artist through working with a model that was not able to be a model. In 2011 the project *Ik zie ik zie wat jij niet ziet* (I see, I see, what you can't see) took place in Blauwbörgje, a home for people with dementia in Groningen. The ten students that applied for this project were each to portray a person with dementia in the common rooms of the institution. The process was guided by visual artist Herman van Hoogdalem. Before the project, Hoogdalem had always made a clear separation between his work as a teacher at the academy and his work as an artist, in which he created, amongst other things, large paintings of people with dementia.[11] This project allowed him to bring both aspects together. He let the students enter the world he knew as an artist and granted them the same kind of encounter he had experienced. He knew that the human relationship would profoundly affect the artistic relationship in this process. Students at an art school are familiar with the classic practice of drawing from a model, which then results in a portrait that can be exhibited. The paid models take on a coded position as an object to be used for art. They agree that their physical characteristics and appearance might be transformed by the artist in order to create the work the artist has in mind. The model is the motivation. The artist is the directive. These are two agreed upon positions. The model gets paid. The artist gets an image.

However, when the drawing takes place within a social context in which it is impossible to objectify the model, the student has no choice but to adopt a different attitude. There is no posing to speak of, if only for the reason that it is unclear whether a person with dementia can and wants to take up this position or not. Frequently, the students were sent away because the model did not feel like it that day. In addition, it is impossible to objectify a person with dementia because, depending on which stage they are in, they cannot or only partially succeed in doing this themselves. A very human aspect breaks into the realm of the artistic practice precisely because a person with dementia possesses a kind of honesty that is foreign to other people. However, sometimes this honesty results in a kind of

11
His best-known works can be found in Wanders 2013.

response that evokes so much embarrassment that the individual must be clearly distinguished from the disease. Yet most of the time honesty remains the decisive factor: what you see is what you get. At least, when the model is truly looked at. And that is something these art students are very good at. Because they have such an open and attentive attitude, the students get to see what no other model could reveal. This is moving, confusing, and creates a big responsibility, especially in dealing with that which borders on embarrassment. And of course the question for whom the students are making these portraits keeps coming up. For themselves, because they are allowed to witness something extraordinary? For the world, because they show a special image of dementia? And how could it benefit the model? This dilemma haunts them, and rightly so. To portray people with dementia means to be in a continuous state of doubt. What do you make visible and to whom?

The art students were fully aware of the shift that occurred within the artistic space created here. They understood that these people were not traditional models, or educational objects that could be used to make beautiful pictures, nor were they clients, but people who could only have an impact on the creation of the portrait through the physical encounter and the human interaction. That is exactly why the students placed themselves across from the person they were appointed to. They sought the encounter, with the portrait as an alibi and outcome. They were not the ones leading the process, the person in front of them was. Because of the art students' open attitude they were able to see what the person with dementia wanted to reveal to them, and another form of portraiture could thus emerge. The encounter between the artist and the person with dementia provided the material for the portrait. The students responded to the unforeseen statements and movements of the person with dementia. While the artistic space that surrounds a person with dementia makes an encounter possible, it is the freedom and space that a person with dementia takes that establishes it. A person with dementia guarantees the unexpected, the new, and the different, to which the artist has learned to be open.

Saskia is impressed by the first meeting with her model. He speaks to her as if she is a garage owner and wants to sell her his car. Following the advice of the Blauwbörgje's employees, she decides not to go against it. Every week he gives her a different role. The last role she also decides to go along with is the role of his wife. 'Bye sweetheart, 'till next time...' She starts writing. A series of concise, sharp stories are created in this way. Saskia discovers that she can write and that she can combine this newfound ability with her drawings.[12]

One of the other students explains:

I find it so painful to see how she talks, but that nobody is listening. There are eight people in the living room, she is sitting in the middle of it and the others are completely ignoring her. So I decide to listen to her attentively. She talks about the chair she is sitting in, it is an important object from her past. I make a drawing of the chair and give it to her. Two weeks later I come into the room and she asks if I want to sit in her chair. She has pinned the drawing to the wall. She moves me, I realize that I'm a lot like her, I'm not a social creature, and when I draw her now, I create more and more space around her. She is alone.[13]

The artistic space creates the possibility to view not just the person with dementia differently, but also of their surroundings. The presence of the students and the space created by portraying them breaks into the institution's public domain, in which social interaction is dominated by the capabilities of the person with dementia.

[12]
Observation Herman van Hoogdalem.

[13]
From a conversation between a student and Herman van Hoogdalem. See also: Coumans en Van Hoogdalem 2016.

The Useless, Fragile and Non-productive Space

The artistic enters the space of dementia's institutional care context even more than it enters its social environment. The project took place within the context of an institution that works according to a functionality and protocol that have their roots in economic principles; the so-called system world of Habermas in which all actions are both strategical and instrumental. Not the encounter as an uncertain act, but caring for as a goal-oriented action is the institutional maxim for the caretakers. Within this environment, a space was introduced in which different principles prevailed. In a lecture in 2006, Jacques Rancière spoke of the importance of spaces and places that are–in the words of the artists of Campement urbain–'extremely useless, fragile and non-productive'.[14] He used a project by a group of French artists who call themselves Campement urbain to illustrate this. The group created a silent space in one of the most notorious neighbourhoods of Paris. Only one person at a time could sit in this quiet room, and therefore this person was, for a moment, alone but also connected to others. For this reason the artists called the project *I and Us* (*Moi et Nous*). The importance of these kinds of spaces lies in the fact that they create both the possibility of being separated from and connected to their environments. In these spaces something other may occur that could affect the space that surround them. In the project discussed in Rancière's lecture the solitary meditation resulted in choosing a statement that was subsequently propagated by printing it on a T-shirt. In *I see, I see what you can't see* a different kind of silent space of reflection was created within the functional space of taking care of people. Students took the caretakers and relatives along in their alternate way of looking at the person with dementia. A kind of silence and meditation arose that bore similarities to the experience of sitting in the silent room in Rancière's example. The student's view can influence the onlooker's view even before the portrait is

14
Rancière 2006.

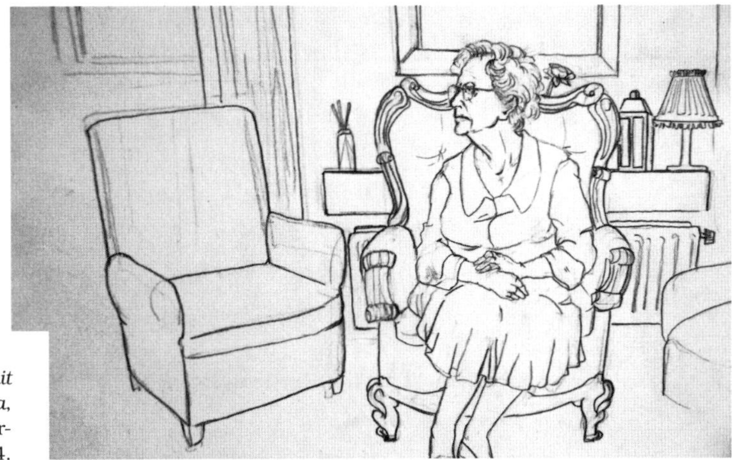

Maroussia Jansen, *Portrait of Woman with Dementia*, Groningen, the Netherlands, 2014.

displayed and hangs on the wall of the Blauwbörgje as exhibition art. The artistic space starts with how the students see their surroundings and the drawings they create as a result. The interaction took place in how the artistic view and the view from outside of art intersect and question each other during the extensive discussion sessions that were held every week after working on the portraits. It is great that after these sessions there was an exhibition with portraits that provided several personal views of people with dementia, and that they were not just seen as a group with a disease, but as individuals who, from their unorthodox behaviours and the free space they naturally occupy, are able to reveal something other than what we already know. The actual work, however, was already done by then.

Just as in the *Academy of the People* project and Bart Lodewijks' work, a different perspective emerged in *I see, I see what you can't see*. There was room for entirely new conversations that are just as important as the resulting image, which raises the question of what actually is the artistic work. I would say it is the total of the artistic act and the artistic product that, through its exhibition, becomes a type of act on its own. If there is such a thing as a 'public', it is involved in both the creation of the images and in their exposition. The portraits of *I see, I see* were

ART AS ENCOUNTER

exhibited at the academy as well as at the institution, and the variety of portraits provided the public with many opportunities to assimilate a different image of dementia.

Hannah Arendt's description of the public space as the space of a variety of perspectives[15] is reflected in this project because ten portrait sessions were taking place simultaneously.

15
Arendt, 1958, p. 57, 58.

Conclusion

Art is able to situate itself into life's daily affairs not just as a product or an image, but also as an artistic space in which a different practice and attitude become visible. Artists settle there and it is their presence, their view, and their manner of acting that make it an artistic visual space. The projects described here are small, intimate projects that foreground the exchange between people, not the presentation to the general public. The public, the other person, is involved in the realization of the artwork from the beginning. In that sense, the projects could be called 'encounter art' as discussed in *Relational Aesthetics*. The interaction with the audience is part of the artwork and/or the artistic practice. However (and here I believe is where the practice differs from Rancière's example of Campement urbain), the artist retains control over his artistic process. The artistic process has moved from the studio, the traditional site of creation, to society, or rather to concrete contexts with specific publics: the local residents, the shoppers at Ikea, the officers at the police station, and the people living in the healthcare facility. Yet art is a catalyst that manages to draw the public into a space in which the non-productive, the fragile, and the useless call the shots. The artistic process has thus become an artistic research process that examines new possibilities together with the other.

CRISIS, ART AND THEIR MULTIPLE AUDIENCES
From Embros Theatre to IDAMM

Eva Fotiadi

Art appears to be thriving in Athens over the last six years of ongoing crisis, austerity, and protest. Events such as the occupation of the Embros Theatre (2011), or the 4th Athens Biennale (2013) mobilized more people than the organizers ever dreamt of. For brief moments, such projects seemed to also bring the art world closer to the 'real' world of citizens' self-organized resistance to the crisis. During the same period, the international contemporary art world seemed to find Greece particularly interesting too. For instance, half the upcoming Documenta 14 (2017) will take place in Athens under the working title 'Learning from Athens'. Ai Weiwei has set up a studio on the island of Lesvos. Jan Fabre was appointed artistic director of the Greek Festival; albeit that his proposed programme caused such an outcry that he resigned a week later.

Both in and outside of Greece some have said that this spring of artistic activity, engagement and an interweaving of art and 'real' life has been a form of people's resistance to crisis and precarization. The arts are regarded as performing the function of a public sphere fostering democracy, or even as offering experimental economic models.[1] All this is part and parcel of a strikingly asymmetrical international reception of Greece by different worlds: while the Greek crisis and anti-austerity protests are mostly discussed negatively in the world of mainstream politics, economy and media, they are treated with respect in mainstream contemporary arts and in academia.[2]

The first part of this essay is a selection of episodes from artistic or discursive events that relate to art and crisis in Greece. In the second part, I elaborate on some thoughts about them. Most episodes relate to the expansion of artists' and citizens' collective self-organization and participation in bottom-up, cultural, social, political as well as entrepreneurial initiatives.[3] The essay serves no central argument or conclusion, because the situation discussed here has not yet reached any kind of closure. The analysis in the second part focuses on three central themes, and

[1] See, e.g., Tsiara 2015; Panagiotara and Tsintziloni 2015; Karaba 2013.

[2] See, e.g., Kuhnt 2012; Donadio 2011; Beauvallet 2016.

[3] See, e.g., Blisset 2013; Goudouna 2014; Panagiotara and Tsintziloni 2015; Tsiara 2015.

is divided into three sections accordingly. First, the rise of collectivity has marked the discourse of people's active resistance against crisis and austerity.[4] As I will maintain, 'collectivity' became a kind of dispositif with which the distinction between active agents and passive audiences, as well as that between social, political and artistic praxis appeared to become blurry, and this blurriness came to serve various functions. Second, as collectives gained public visibility and were encouraged from various sides to continue their often conceived as temporary initiatives ad infinitum, an undeclared transformation occurred. Namely, what had started as politicized intervention or participation in public life seemed to turn to a performance of labour, more akin to the mode of precarious labour in neoliberal economy as described by Maurizio Lazzarato, than to a mode of resistance against it. In the last section, the discussion returns to the question of the international (or better, the European) art world and its preoccupation with the Greek crisis. So far, this preoccupation has been expressed through an interest less in art works that are representative of the situation than in staging panels with participants representing people's resistance against it. The essay closes with a plea for strategically drawing art out of the blurriness of this undifferentiated art and crisis discourse, as a way of giving art a function of creating distance, in order to decide upon one's priorities for the future.

My own position as a Greek living abroad since thirteen years, as well as my current research in contemporary artistic interventions in urban space in Athens, make me a sort of simultaneously distant and involved observer. The selected episodes render this position explicit. The approach is largely empirical, as I am myself implicated in several of the audiences I refer to. Additionally, I draw rather unsystematically from recorded and unrecorded discussions, all of which are kept anonymous.

The episodes I talk about began in 2011. The conventional starting point of the situation they refer to should rather

4

See, e.g., Blisset 2013; CommonsFest 2016.

be placed in 2008. In Greece, the December of that year was marked by violent, massive riots following the shooting of a 15-year-old boy by a policeman in Athens, and these riots spread all over the country. Globally, 2007/2008 was the beginning of a succession of financial crises. The rise of people's collective self-organization and new forms of political and creative protest (e.g. the Occupy movement) are not local, but global phenomena of recent years. Even though this essay focuses narrowly on Greece, I agree that a broader contextualization is also important.

Part I

AMSTERDAM/ATHENS, NOVEMBER 2011: EMBROS THE-ATRE. My Facebook and email accounts are bombarded with announcements about a 'reactivation' of the Embros Theatre in Athens. More and more friends share photos and updates on a daily basis. Despite a busy life in Amsterdam it is impossible to resist opening posts. Something different from the regular Greek crisis and protest news is happening. The since 2007 abandoned theatre Embros was reactivated by the so-called Mavili Collective. They were an alliance of young practitioners and theorists mainly of performance between theatre and visual arts, an art that had no institutional place in the Greek art and theatre landscape.[5] Embros is located in the downtown district of Psyrri, which is heavily gentrified by the leisure indus-tries. A group of Psyrri residents also supported the reactivation. To avoid their project being identified with existing subcultures in the Athenian scene, Mavili invited a mix of young, starting artists, alongside famous and successful ones, to present work in progress. They also consciously selected their vocabulary, foregrounding 'reactivation' to 'squatting' or 'occupation'.[6] Several people I know contributed to the twelve days of Embros' reac-tivation with anything from performance and workshops to making coffee. Some became involved through artists'

[5] See, e.g., Mavili Collective 2012; Mavili Collective 2014; [MacGraw] 2015; Free Self-managed Embros Theatre; Argyropoulou 2012.

[6] Argyropoulou 2012, p. 57.

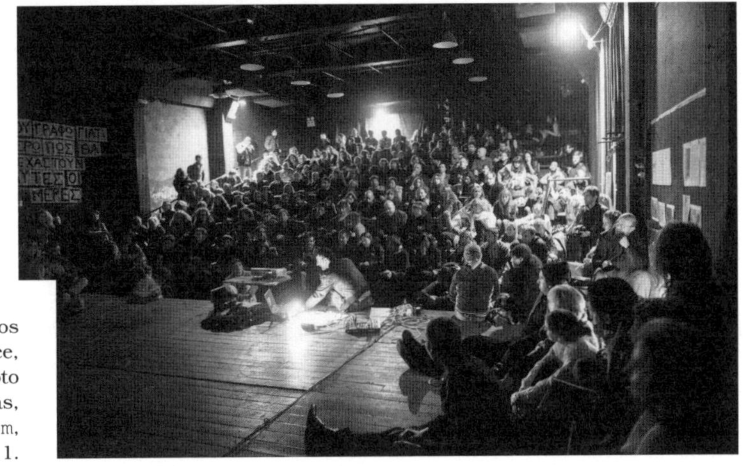

Re-activation of Embros Theatre, Athens, Greece, November 2011. © Photo by Georgios Makkas, www.gmakkas.com, 2011.

groups they were loosely connected to. Throughout the twelve evenings the theatre was packed. The ambitious, autonomous, collective, aesthetically pluralistic and playful, performative gesture of claiming a space for art beyond existing institutions and established artistic circles, reached beyond a specialized performance audience. At the end of the twelve days, the Mavili Collective members realized that the theatre's reactivation had become an event that exceeded their artistic agenda. They decided to invite anyone interested, individual or collective and not necessarily from the arts, to participate in an open weekly assembly that would decide how to run the theatre through horizontal processes. From an artistic experiment, Embros was turned into a mixed artistic, political, and social one. It cancelled dividing lines between makers and audiences, the artistic and the political; it welcomed dissonance, making everyone a potential stakeholder and any activity potentially possible. From the beginning, the assembly was a disaster. Tensions and fights abounded. Soon after, the Mavili Collective dissolved. Nonetheless, Embros continues its operation to this day, despite several attempts by authorities to close it down, and with different people in the assembly.

OCTOBER–NOVEMBER 2013: AB4 AGORA & SYNATHINA. At the end of September 2013. the 4th edition of the Athens

          CRISIS, ART AND THEIR MULTIPLE AUDIENCES

Biennale (AB4) entitled AGORA opened its doors at the Old Athens Stock Exchange with as central theme the question: 'Now what?' A traditional exhibition is shown on the two upper floors, but the real heart of AGORA is the central hall of the old Stock Exchange. There, for two whole months, daily events took place: performances, lectures, workshops, project presentations, a conference, music concerts, and even an opera performance. Characteristic for AB4 was that nobody had a curatorial overview of the programme. During the previous winter the directors of the biennale had initiated meetings in Athens with artists, curators, theorists and practitioners in the creative industries to brainstorm about the upcoming edition. This collective preparation process was born out of necessity rather than choice. However, it had the interesting result of evolving into a curatorial group of as many as 42 members, all of whom could invite participants. Together with artist Nikos Doulos we edited the online reader *Event as Process: Cities in an Ongoing State of Emergency and the Artists' Stance*, following an invitation to contribute to the theory programme.[7] Moreover, there were two open calls to which anyone could submit a proposal online. Proposals were made permanently visible on AB4's website and a few were included in AGORA's programme.[8] Again, anyone could change from audience to contributor by submitting a proposal, they did not need to be professionals. The innumerable events saw returning audiences. Live-streaming enabled home attendance, though quality was often only fair. This curatorial format resonated with the times. In private conversations sceptics maintained that the organizers only cared about the continuous presence of people in the central hall, about the image of activity and openness, rather than about content. Anyhow, AGORA was successful overall in foregrounding the variety of collective initiatives internationally, in introducing innovative collective and voluntary curating, and it received more attention from abroad than any previous edition. A year later, the Athens Biennale and the Visual

BEING PUBLIC

Culture Research Centre from war-ridden Kiev received the Princess Margriet Award of the European Cultural Foundation 'for their work building on the public sphere, creating sorely needed open space for artistic imagination'.[9]

About 250 meters west of AGORA's site, Athenian collectives were presented with another stage while AB4 was running. On October 11th 2013, the mayor of Athens inaugurated a 'roof' for the formerly digital platform SynAthina.[10] Official and unofficial citizens groups were invited to register. The platform provided them with a space for public visibility and events, networking between the citizens groups and by organizing logistical support particularly from the municipal bureaucracy. In 2015, the Municipality of Athens was among the five winners of Mayor's Challenge, a European innovation competition organized by Bloomberg Philanthropies, an organization of Mike Bloomberg, former mayor of New York. Bloomberg's organization sponsors and researches the implementation of small scale projects that improve the quality of life in cities.[11]

ATHENS, FEBRUARY 2015: ASSEMBLIES. I am in Athens for three weeks to continue my research. Similarly to other such trips in previous years, I contact people I would like to talk to. This time there is something new. Some suggest I could better join the 'x' or 'y' assembly and we can also organize a one-to-one meeting. From the Netherlands I am used to work meetings that last one to two hours and decide on majority rule. The Athenian assemblies of collective self-organized artistic or other initiatives I visited were open to everyone; they started at least one hour late; they lasted a minimum of three hours; and they reached decisions only by consensus. In assemblies of art-related events or structures, participants were not only professionals from the arts. The step from viewer to producer still seemed easy, if not normalized. Yet especially those assemblies that ere linked to long-term structures—such as the Embros assembly—were not characterized by positive energy or a pleasant atmosphere.

9
European Cultural
Foundation 2015.

10
www.synathina.gr.

11
Bloomberg Philanthropies
2014.

     CRISIS, ART AND THEIR MULTIPLE AUDIENCES

BERLIN, SEPTEMBER 2015–FEBRUARY 2016: GREEK-PANEL FATIGUE. A nightmarish summer for Greek political and civil life has come to an end with an outcome characterized by many as a coup d'état. The German government played a prominent role. In September, in Berlin the new season starts with artistic and discursive events in cultural and academic institutions. From the beginning of September until Christmas 2015, hardly a single week went by without at least one event either about Greece, from Greece, or with Greek participants representing in some capacity the situation in Greece. I recall watching Greek journalists, visual artists, theatre directors, film makers, cultural managers, academics, literary authors, activists and ex-politicians appearing in public events at theatres such as HAU, Gorki, Volksbühne, TAK, Neuköllner Oper, Sophiensaele, and other cultural venues, such as the Akademie der Künste, Savvy Contemporary, or Topographie des Terrors. All events were well attended, often full. Audiences varied depending upon each event's organizers and hosting institution. Berlin's critical artistic, intellectual and activist scene was usually represented. The majority of these events were, or included, panel discussions, which were added to innumerable TV panels since the summer. One evening at Gorki an organizer and participant of many such events mentioned a friend's complain about 'Greek-panel fatigue'.

In early 2016, the supply slowed down. A couple of highlights were the theatre piece *Graecomania 200 Years* (HAU), a German production, and the public launch of ex-Greek minister of Finance Yannis Varoufakis' new political movement DiEM25 at the Volksbühne. It followed earlier appearances of Varoufakis at Volksbühne with Bifo and at London's Royal Festival Hall with Slavoj Žižek and Julian Assange.

ATHENS, NOVEMBER 2015. AB5-6 OMONOIA. Back to Athens for my research and for the opening of AB5-6. The Athens Biennale opened its 5th and 6th editions combined under the title OMONOIA (Concorde) and in collaboration with the Municipality of Athens. It is based again in a deserted building, the late nineteenth-century Baggeion Hotel at Omonia Square. AB5-6 will run slowly over two years. Again with collective processes but this time with a single 'programme director' (not curator), a London-based anthropologist from the academic world, new to the local context. OMONOIA's initial twelve-day programme is

> an ongoing collective experiment that will transform the Omonoia area into a social laboratory of ideas with the contribution of anthropologists, researchers, activists, academics, artists, civic organisations and self-managed groups.[12]

12
Athens Biennale 2015.

The budget is unclear. The Baggeion has no functioning toilets or heating and it floods after heavy rains. The first day started with an international conference. On the second day, closed working groups of invited local and foreign artistic and activist collectives took place in the morning. In the afternoon, an open to the public assembly received and discussed ideas produced by the working groups. Through these processes the next step of AB5-6 should be planned. The second day was well attended by representatives of foreign art and non-art activist collectives who, according to one of my research interviewees, were wondering where the peer groups that they knew from the local scene had gone.

BERLIN, DECEMBER 2016. DOCUMENTA 14 MAGAZINE LAUNCH *SOUTH AS A STATE OF MIND*. One of the highlights in the Berlin cultural scene's intense engagement with Greece, was the launch of the first issue of Documenta 14 magazine *South as a State of Mind*. Originally this was the magazine of Kunsthalle Athena, Documenta's official local host in Athens. The programme of two hours included short speeches, lectures, project presentations, live music and screenings. The venue was packed. Two elements distinguished this event from any other I have personally attended in Berlin and which linked to Greece. First, except for two contributions that referred to Greece, I can only recall presentations that were about post- or neo-colonialism in *Réunion* Island, Morocco, Nigeria, and if I remember correctly, also India or Algeria. Most of the live music was jazz. Second, no time for questions or discussion was given to the audience, only during the after party.

BERLIN/ATHENS, FEBRUARY 2016. IDAMM. A Facebook page circulates and receives multiple likes. It is the page of the so-called Institute for the Management of the Athenian Post-documenta Melancholy (IDAMM), and it includes only one text. Below here I quote some extracts:

> Athens is not being instrumentalized as a general example of failure, but as some sort of paradigm that has something to teach. The ignorant will become teachers, Greek artists will sell like hot cakes in the art markets and they will finally get to participate in exhibitions abroad (what more do the Lebanese have after all?). ...
>
> However there are also those who, unable to see the larger picture, bear the lyrical plea of resistance, so familiar and so quaint to all of us by now. Through spiteful reactions to what they call the neo-colonial, exoticist, hegemonic existence of the Documenta, they mock the intentions of the organization, claiming that the indigenous artistic subjects are being reduced to trivago (`www.trivago.com`) by the professional art tourists, and so on. ...
>
> Through what processes and from which starting point is the image of a creative periphery of the crisis constructed? Are there or will there be antagonistic practices between the Documenta and the local institutions? Who owns the crisis, and who will eventually manage to showcase it, to represent it and to benefit from it the most? ...

[IDAMM] aims to function as an observatory of this event, to study and understand … In order to meet the special needs of this challenging project, IDAMM will deploy all these innovative ideas and all the new scientific, activist, artistic and other cross-disciplinary practices that will result from flexible collaborations, with anyone who will be deemed suitable to support the Institute in this difficult venture.[13]

13
Institute for the Management of the Athenian Post-documenta Melancholy 2016.

Part II

Collectivity and Participation

I began with the reactivation of Embros in the first part, because it was a small turning point between the past and what has followed. It was the moment when the long-standing aesthetic-political stakes of young artists and intellectuals for new spaces, institutions and relations met and resonated with the social and political stakes of a broad range of citizens wanting institutional changes in Greece. To be more precise, since the beginning of the 2000s, a few dispersed group initiatives for artistic projects had started appearing in Athens. Many of them were formed as a way of realizing projects that went beyond the interests or ambitions of existing institutions.[14] After the mid-2000s, collectives began to multiply significantly, but December 2008 and the economic recession gave them a decisive boost. These Greek artistic collectives were, and to the extent of my knowledge often still are, flexible, interdisciplinary, horizontal alliances of individuals who mostly maintain their individual careers, and may also be involved in more than one collective. In the various instances that had mobilized masses of people into action and protest since the riots of December 2008, an organizational culture and political sensorium of collectivity had been nurtured. Citizens started neighbourhood initiatives, anti-poverty initiatives, collectives in industrial production, in solidarity economy and urban agriculture, social pharmacies, social clinics, and so on.[15] Some came

14
See, for instance, Filopappou Group (2001–), Locus Athens (2004–), Athens Biennale (2005–), Mavili Collective (2010–), a.o.

15
About citizens' solidarity initiatives, see e.g. Petropoulou 2013; Petropoulou 2014; Vaiou and Kalandides 2015.

     CRISIS, ART AND THEIR MULTIPLE AUDIENCES

to exist, became visible or in got into contact with one another through the Syntagma Occupation of summer 2011.[16] The reactivation of Embros was initially an artistic collective's initiative (Mavili Collective) that brought to the fore and made visible a multitude of other artistic collective formations and collaborations. In Embros they became more conscious of their energy and potential. The continuation of the theatre's operation after the first twelve days, and the establishment of the weekly general assembly, brought in more individuals and collectives. They were the direct and indirect audiences of the initial twelve days, who did not necessarily work in the arts.

Consequently, in the new distribution of roles and places at the theatre and the assembly, the space of the stage and the space behind the stage, as well as the time of the performance and the time before and after the performance, were opened up to members of the performance art's audience, but also of the broader public. In her book, *Social Works,* the American performance scholar Shannon Jackson maintains that particularly performance—which is historically a collective, interdisciplinary practice and requires human planning, coordination, and management in time and space—can 'contribute to interdependent social imaginings'.[17] This quite idealistic approach seemed to find a radical materialization when the Embros assembly opened up the experiment, *as well as* the visibility offered by the theatrical apparatus and Mavili Collective's success, to anyone who wanted to participate. The only requirement was that they acknowledged the occupation of Embros as a 'common good'. Moreover, as Sozita Goudouna pointed out,

> [T]he vital imperative for the assembly [was] to be part of a wider network of similar collectivities (occupations, groups, collectives, and individuals) to foster a transnational network of solidarity by exploring common ground of possible collaborations.[18]

16
See, e.g., Papadopoulos, Tsianos, and Tsomou 2012.

17
Jackson 2011, p. 14.

18
Goudouna 2014, p. 87.

During the first years of resistance to the crisis, 'collectivity' seemed to fill the space of the social, political and affective vacuum that the crumbling institutions were leaving behind. This rise of collectivity and respective discourses of 'the commons,' 'communities' et cetera, were, of course, part of the broader global rise of social protests and occupy movements, from New York to Madrid and from Kiev to Istanbul, not to mention the Arab Spring. Specifically in the daily experience of the Greek crisis—the context that I am familiar with—the collective became a kind of dispositif that served multiple functions: it fulfilled people's need to feel some comfort in togetherness and solidarity in the face of increasing precarization in daily life; it fulfilled the urge 'to do something' in response to a state of emergency that had been emphatically promoted by governmental policies and the media since the riots of 2008;[19] it filled people's time with something meaningful when professional activities slowed down; it opened a new field of political representation, participation and experience of democracy when these became extinct in state politics.

Michel Foucault explains how in his use, the term 'dispositif' (sometimes translated in English as 'apparatus'), also expresses a sort of 'formation which has as its major function at a given historical moment that of responding to an *urgent need*. The apparatus thus has a dominant strategic function.'[20] This could indeed be maintained about collectivity and the collective in the Greek discourse of crisis and resistance. Regardless of how well (or not) they worked in practice, collective initiatives and actions captured the imagination and expressed the ideology as well as the ethics and aesthetics of a wide range of citizens: from the anarchists of the Exarcheia district to the conservative bourgeoisie of Kolonaki, and from the fascists of the Golden Dawn organization to the newly politicized art scene.

The reactivation of Embros Theatre was neither the first, nor the only occasion that brought artists' groups and

     CRISIS, ART AND THEIR MULTIPLE AUDIENCES

---

[19] Fotiadi 2016.

[20] Foucault 1977, p. 195.

collectives together. For example, in 2009, the 2nd Athens Biennale featured *Live*, a part of the exhibition curated by a choreographer and a visual artist, which included live activities undertaken also by artists' groups. Later, in June 2012, a three-days meeting entitled *Systems* was organized by the cultural space CAMP, which featured about 46 artists' groups and collectives. Since 2013, the parallel programme of the Athenian art fair Art Athina hosts the *Platforms Project* for local and international groups. However, only in Embros the collectives were not only hosted but were also the hosts, and the established division between actors and audiences, between the performance of art and of politics, gave way to a different aesthetico-political paradigm and sensorium that momentarily captured the imagination of a broader public. It gained such emblematic significance that despite the disastrous experience of the assembly's actual operation, it still maintains its lure today and the theatre has even become a tourist attraction.

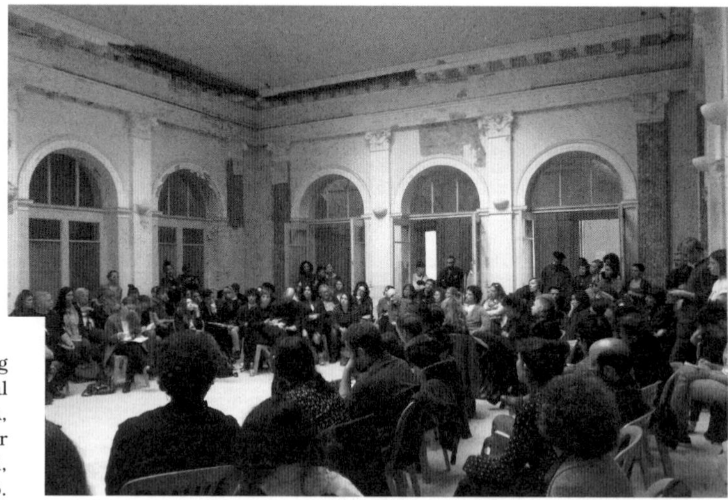

General assembly, opening days of Athens Biennial editions 5-6 OMONOIA, Athens, Greece, November 2015. Photo by Eva Fotiadi, 2015.

Participation and Labour

So what happens when the artists, the audience and the public, after having taken the stage of the theatre and the assembly through the dispositif of the collective, are invited onto other stages, such as AB4 AGORA or SynAthina? In these examples the activity of collectives was given institutional recognition, public visibility, a platform to present themselves and their work and to network and discuss. SynAthina also provided assistance with bureaucracy. Importantly, while at the occupied Embros Theatre or in some earlier occupations (e.g., the Opera House, Navarino Park, Syntagma Square, or ERT-open), self-organized artists and/or citizens seized the respective stages themselves, in AB4 or SynAthina they were invited on stage, and were hosted and framed. Consequently, the political performative gesture of collectively taking the stage and self-organizing gave way to a performance of immaterial and unpaid labour—brainstorming, organizing, communicating and networking. In order to reflect upon certain consequences for this transition, let me take a closer look at the statements and open calls of the two examples, against the backdrop of Bojana Kunst's analysis of the production of subjectivity and sociality in the labour of performing artists and participating audiences.

According to the central statement on AGORA's homepage, AB4 '[could not] but respond to the bleak situation' of the financial crisis. It responded 'through a pertinent question: now what?'[21] AGORA was conceived as a 'collaborative process in producing an exhibition', as a place for 'exchange', 'interaction' and 'critique' where thinking 'entail[ed] rupture, judgement and conflict'. Moreover, it was related to notions of 'the assembly and the assemblage', as a 'succession of objects, collaborative events, performances, roundtable discussions, film screenings, workshops and educational programs', a 'collective experiment … between professionals from different backgrounds', who shared 'a sense of responsibility and an urge to co-produce meaning'. In the AB4 team's open call 'everyone who seeks to develop operational approaches and attitudes in today's critical time' [was] invited to contribute with 'creative support'. So, as a whole, this call foregrounded notions of collaboration, collective activity, communication, creativity and responsibility.

21
Doulos and Fotiadi 2013 for all quotations in this paragraph.

       CRISIS, ART AND THEIR MULTIPLE AUDIENCES

A few weeks later, in the much less elaborated public announcement of the inauguration of SynAthina's new building, similar traits of urgency, collectivity, action, communication and responsibility were underlined. Emphasis was placed on 'groups of citizens', that 'relate to each other around solutions and actions for the good of their neighbourhood or the city'.[22] Sole criterion for registration with the platform was their 'active involvement in activities for the common good'. The platform is still active and provides possibilities for 'broader communication, information about past actions, peer exchange of experience and expertise'. SynAthina also provides logistical support when dealing with municipal bureaucracy. As I mentioned in Part I, both the Biennale and the Municipality of Athens received international awards by ECF and Bloomberg Philanthropies for AGORA and SynAthina, respectively. In 2015, they joined forces as co-organizers of OMONOIA (2015–2017).

Following Maurizio Lazzarato's analysis of labour in relation to political subjectification, the philosopher and performance theorist Bojana Kunst discusses the notion of 'the production of subjectivity'. With Lazzarato, she maintains that it is more pertinent than 'immaterial labor' or 'cognitive labor' in describing traits of contemporary capitalism.[23] Subjectivity is 'the single largest commodity that we produce, because it goes into the production of all other commodities'.[24] It is characterized by 'creativity, imagination and dynamism', human powers on which contemporary society places great emphasis and that are now becoming standardized, normalized and intertwined with self-governance.[25] This happens as the labour market and state social welfare have been destabilized and individuals feel insecure about their work and their future well-being. Consequently, contemporary subjects find themselves in an ongoing need to be flexible, transformable, to keep their presence and action visible and communicable among peers. Thought, language and creativity

23
Kunst 2015, p. 19.

24
Lazzarato in ibid.

25
Ibid.

become primary tools for the production of value. Similarly to other theorists of the arts, such as Pascal Gielen or Marion van Osten,[26] Kunst sees a close proximity between artists' labour and capitalism: 'the performer becomes the ideal virtuoso worker for contemporary capitalism, producing communication through the means of communication: the means are the language and actions of the body'.[27]

Collectives demonstrate the traits described by Lazzarato and Kunst. To address crisis and precarization, they appear creative and imaginative in inventing solutions and structures. They show dynamism and restless activity in addition to, or in place of, their previous daily routines. The forms and expansion of communication and collaboration play a crucial role both internally (e.g., in assemblies, in the distribution of tasks) and externally (among peers). The production of collectivity as crisis resistance can be seen as the production of collective subjectivities that have emerged as emergency structures between the domains of the private (e.g., family, friends) and the public (e.g., the neighbourhood, the city). Collective, mostly voluntary initiatives were usually conceived as temporary solutions[28] and even as opposition to dysfunctional, collapsing or corrupted institutions.

Awarding such initiatives had double consequences. On the one hand, the awards encouraged a prolongation ad infinitum of what had emerged as people's emergency reaction, often intended as temporary, but without directly offering them the means to turn the voluntary work into paid labour. On the other hand, direct material and other support went to the hosting institutions of the Athens Biennale and Athens Municipality, which had staged the force of collectives, but did not change their own core structures and hierarchies as response to collectivity's call (something that Mavili Collective had, for instance, done by replacing itself with an open assembly at Embros). Yet the awarded institutions themselves remained no less dependent and

CRISIS, ART AND THEIR MULTIPLE AUDIENCES

---

26 See, e.g., Gielen and De Bruyne 2009; Van Osten et al. 2007.

27 Kunst 2015, p. 31.

28 Vaiou and Kalandidis 2015.

precarious than anyone else: their awards came with the imperative to continue on the same path. The institutions became vehicles for the prolongation and normalization of the emergency artistic and social structures of unpaid labour, sometimes even concealing collective oppositional attitudes under the brand of responsible citizenship. A brand consecrated by institutional agents (ECF, Bloomberg Philanthropies) with well-defined places in international hierarchies and networks of power. In essence, the awards consolidated Lazzarato's identification of the production of subjectivity in crisis as production of value in neoliberalism.

Besides the production of subjectivity, Bojana Kunst also discusses another kind of production of value through labour that is performed within contemporary art institutions: the production of sociality. Two aspects of her analysis interest me here: the first concerns the effort of audiences that are called to participate to artistic events, especially in the visual arts; the second concerns collaborative artists' work.

In participatory events the audience is called to interact, talk, express opinions, move, play, eat, and so on. This effort produces forms of sociality that actually resemble the production of subjectivity discussed above: they involve cognitive, creative, social and affective abilities of the audience as constitutive elements of the live event. The effort is usually not major. Nonetheless, it is this effort that lends added value to the art events and institutions for becoming active, social spaces. AGORA and SynAthina indeed gained their value from being seen as such spaces. Kunst's approach to the effort of participating audiences finds a double application here. First, through the open calls, the platforms addressed their audiences: anyone reached by the call, people the organizers didn't know and who may or may not be professional cultural or social workers. Secondly, by inviting collectives in general, they indirectly invited all those people who, through the dispositif of collectivity with open participation, had turned from passive audiences into active agents.

In addressing the question whether the investment of effort by the art audience is a form of exploitation, Kunst suggests that to answer it one should reflect on the fact that

> the audience of contemporary artistic institutions is no longer organized through the dispositive of watching (the passive observation of individuals) … Rather, the audience seems like a disorganized sum of fleeting and impermanent gestures, alliances, attractions, repulsions, agreements … the role of the artistic event is that of capturing the life force of such a multitude and performing it as 'the public', in the fact that the audience provides the event with the political, social and affective dimension.[29]

29
Kunst 2015, p. 62.

Indeed, the large number, great diversity and the rhizomatic emergence of collective initiatives in Athens render their description as a multitude quite relevant. And it is exactly the performance of this multitude as a 'public' that turns international attention to the platforms that stage this multitude, as representative of society's resistance against the crisis. As I mentioned in the introduction, it is sometimes maintained that the arts have been functioning as a public sphere during the Greek crisis. I would share here Bojana Kunst's reservations that, especially when participatory events abound, by blurring the borders between the audience and the work, and by equalling the audience with the public, 'an erasure of the ability to judge takes place, which also enables the transformation of our social abilities into the unity of the spectacle'.[30]

30
Ibid., p. 71.

Finally, the production of sociality is also found in artists' collaborative work. Artists know very well that collaborations are crucial for the visibility of their work. Moreover, collaboration in artistic and other types of labour has been fetishized since the 1990s, often because of collective creativity, or the appearance of lack of hierarchies. Nonetheless, artists as much as anyone involved in

          CRISIS, ART AND THEIR MULTIPLE AUDIENCES

collective work can testify that collaboration is awesome, but can at the same time also be extremely difficult and time-consuming and may disguise hierarchies and inequalities under the desire or illusion of a shared 'we'. Additionally, among volunteering subjects, it may simply be difficult to keep the momentum and vision collectively alive. This was sometimes my feeling during the assemblies of long-term collectives with impressive work, which I visited in February 2015. Self-reflection, tiredness, doubt, repetition, may have played a role in why mature local collectives were not strongly represented during OMONOIA's open assembly.

Theory and Art

So what does the international art and performance world as audience of art and crisis in Athens see? What is the role there of ex-viewers who, through the dispositif of collectivity, became doers? And that of remaining viewers who attend artistic and discursive events?

During the long winter semester of Berlin's education on the Greek situation by cultural institutions, there was a striking lack of balance between presentations of artistic or theatrical works and panel discussions. Panels prevailed. They provided a barrage of reports from the front (subjects' direct experience of the situation) and of theoretical approaches (issues of debtocracy, democracy, activism, alongside those of neo-colonialism, dispossession, exoticism, hegemony, radical populism mentioned in Documenta's magazine launch and IDAMM's text). It should come as no surprise that Varoufakis' public appearances at Berlin and London theatres were popular among critical artists and intellectuals. He combined experience from the front, a leftist approach, interdisciplinary theory, excellent performative skills as academic professor, and a call for action. IDAMM's manifesto-like text is also interesting here, because it captures crucial elements of the function of, and reaction to, this international attendance of art and crisis in Greece. In the panels that I followed, Athens was indeed not instrumentalized as a general example of failure, 'but as some sort of paradigm that has something to teach'.[31] In this context the 'image of a creative periphery of the crisis' and the antagonism over the ownership and display of that image were obviously at stake. Crisis was, and still is, being watched. Its image is constructed by what is shown and told.

As I was attending Greek panels in theatre and art venues in Berlin, I was sometimes reminded of a text by Boris Groys entitled 'Under the gaze of theory'. Groys maintains that today's artists, just like every contemporary subject, need a theory to explain what they do first to themselves and then to others. Theory comes *before* art and action, rather than after. In a sense, theory calls subjects to action, it wants to see them move, and thus its call constitutes them as performing subjects. Groys writes:

> If I cease to move I fall off theory's radar—and theory does not like it. Every secular, post-idealistic theory is a call for action. Every critical theory creates a state of urgency—even a state of emergency.[32]

However, this action is not really at the service of any goal external to art and theory. Rather, 'theory calls for action that would perform–and extend–the conditions of theory itself'.[33] The discursive events that I attended, as observatories and as devices that produce theory, were watching the subjects of crisis and art in action. Similarly to ECF or Bloomberg Philanthropies, they, too, were calling upon these subjects to continue performing their action as constitutive parts of the collective subject of crisis. They were calling upon them to demonstrate their critical thinking and creative resistance, both in situ in Athens and at panels abroad. This is why collectives are particularly favoured within a critical art context: they make action more visible, and they make it appear more representable of artists' potential role in social solidarity or political change than the

31
IDAMM 2016.

32
Groys 2012.

33
Ibid.

 CRISIS, ART AND THEIR MULTIPLE AUDIENCES

actions of individuals that may also be seen as personally beneficial and improper of collective dramas. The outcry against Ai Weiwei's photo posing as the dead, Syrian refugee boy on the beach of Lesvos is telling here.

Following the above thoughts, I find myself once again drawn by IDAMM. As response to the sudden international interest in the Athenian art scene, this new institute appropriates the dispositif of watching ('an observatory'), which is both the approach to art and crisis of those supposedly at the audience's position (separate from the stage), as well as that of the traditional aesthetic experience of art and theatre. Yet IDAMM also appropriates the dispositif of collectivity ('flexible collaborations'), the approach to art and crisis of the local, resistance-performing art scene. Theory and activity are being produced, watched and acted upon. There is no audience, because everyone is implicated and busy performing one or more roles. In IDAMM everyone and everything comes together, it contains all positions: a bird's-eye view of the art and crisis situation, and of the war over its image; a call for thought and action; a collective; and, of course, curatorial agency. The production of innovative, flexible, fit-for-the-challenge subjectivities as value production pops up again, since only the suitable will be admitted to this new collective.

IDAMM performs theory and while I don't know who is behind it, I cannot help seeing it as an art project, as one of the most representative works produced by the Greek art scene, as of February 2016. On the one hand, by showing that there are no outside positions, in essence it demonstrates why the Greek crisis is a kind of paradigm that everyone, including the diverse audiences of Berlin's panels and myself as part of them, can learn something from. As a performance of theory it calls us, too, to take action. It constitutes us, its audience, as a heterogeneous collectivity that has something in common to learn, to think, and to do. As an art scholar I write, if I were an artist I could make art, any citizen can join a collective or a movement, for example, Varoufakis' DiEM. If we do it soon, we could also see ourselves circulating on the international stages of the Greek crisis. On the other hand, however, IDAMM as a conceptual art work that appropriates the aesthetics of the international crisis discourse in the worlds of art and academia, shows me to myself as the addressee of theory's call. It creates a temporary exteriority. It makes me stop and contemplate on being addressed, on what I want to be part of, and on how I feel about the crisis becoming hip.

DOES THE TRAGEDY OF THE COMMONS REPEAT ITSELF AS A TRAGEDY OF THE PUBLIC DOMAIN?

Florian Cramer

Gift Economies

'Potlatch' is a traditional Native American gift exchange ceremony. In the twentieth century, the word was adopted for a radical politics and aesthetics of the public domain. The *Lettrist International*, a group of poets, artists and political activists that preceded the Situationist International, published its periodical *Potlatch* free of charge and free of copyright. From 1954 to 1957, *Potlatch* appeared in Paris and the Dutch section of the Situationist International published its own issue of the bulletin in 1959. In an essay included in the Dutch edition, Guy Debord explained gift exchange as a way in which to 'reserve and surmount' the 'negativity' of modern arts.[1] With 'negativity', he not only meant aesthetics, but also economics. The successor to *Potlatch*, the journal *Internationale situationniste*, was free of copyright too. This way, Lettrists and Situationists sought to pre-emptively undermine the collector's and art market's value of their work, at least in theory. In practice, none of the major participants kept up anti-copyright.[2]

Around the same time, in the 1960s, Fluxus sought to fundamentally rethink the economics and public accessibility of art when it focused on street performances and on its own genuine invention 'multiples': the production of artworks (from artists' books to small sculptural objects) in affordable editions. Fluxus' founder and theorist George Maciunas did not literally use the terms 'access' or 'accessibility', yet radically addressed them on both an institutional and aesthetic level. By moving contemporary art from museums and galleries to bookshops and streets, Fluxus sought to give it 'non-elite status in society'.[3] This, by itself, does not differ much from other programmes of bringing art into the public space, for example as open air sculpture. But Maciunas also sought to radically change form and language of contemporary art for this purpose. He wanted art to become 'Vaudeville-art' and 'art-amusement'.[4] Art should become 'simple, amusing, concerned with insignificances, have no commodity or institutional value …

[1] Debord 2007.

[2] Debord, too, published all books that appeared with his author's name under classical copyright.

[3] Maciunas 1971.

[4] Ibid.

obtainable by all and eventually produced by all'.[5] This eventually lead to Fluxus being perceived, like Situationism, as counterculture rather than as contemporary art in its own time. Today, both are mostly seen as forerunners of contemporary performative, conceptualist and political art, although their radical anti-institutional agenda is being overlooked. Little attention has been paid to political-economic visions in both movements: a radical public domain without commodities and private property.

This did not prevent Lettrist, Situationist and Fluxus work from ending up (or even being produced) as collector's items wherever this work had a conventional material form, such as auto- or serigraphs, objects, installations, performance remnants, photographs or original copies of *Potlatch*. When the World Wide Web became a mass medium in the mid-1990s, the first avant-garde and contemporary art that became available online were Situationist writings from the 1960s; works that were conventional text with no collector's value. Thanks to their non-copyright status, they could easily be retyped and uploaded. Works from Fluxus and closely related conceptual and intermedia art movements (including concrete and sound poetry, video and audio art) became the foundation of UbuWeb (`www.ubu.com`). Created in 1996 by poet and conceptual artist Kenneth Goldsmith and still maintained by him today, UbuWeb is the largest online library and electronic archive of avant-garde audio-visual documents. It has become the historically most successful public access initiative for contemporary arts, since it gave artists' books, recordings and videos a public visibility which pre-Internet museums, archives and libraries could not physically provide. In addition, UbuWeb turned this art into a common good since all content of the website is freely and easily downloadable for any Internet user.

This type of public access, however, should not be confused with 'Open Access', the publishing of articles and books as freely available reading materials that, since the 1990s, has become a common practice in academia.[6]

5
Ibid.

6
This book is an Open Access publication, too.

UbuWeb does not comply to the legal requirements and formal criteria for Open Access since it operates in a grey zone of intellectual property. Unlike an Open Access website, UbuWeb neither has formal copyright clearance for all the works it contains, nor does it provide them under formal Open Access usage terms such as those of the Creative Commons licenses (more on them later). What UbuWeb does, however, have in common with the Open Access movement, is that it used the Internet as a catalyst for redefining publishing, from physically limited ownership of material properties to unlimited collective use of non-material goods.

In her 1973 book *Six Years*, art critic Lucy Lippard characterized the performative, conceptualist and intermedia art of the late 1960s and early 1970s as a movement towards the 'dematerialization of the art object'.[7] In 1983, Jean-François Lyotard, founder of postmodernism as a philosophical concept, organized the exhibition *Les Immatériaux* at Centre Pompidou in Paris, which combined art installations by, among others, Daniel Buren and Dan Flavin with extensive displays of scientific inventions and computer technology. If one were to construct a genealogy from Fluxus and conceptual art via Lippard's 'dematerialization' and Lyotard's postmodern 'immaterials' to UbuWeb and the online Situationist text archives, then the latter might be seen as the ultimate realization of 1960s gift economy promises. Promises which, at the time, were still held back by analogue material constraints. Even cheap media such as print have affordances that can be prohibitive: printing, shipping and storage costs, the limited number of print copies versus the unlimited copying of digital files. Live performance art in public spaces was non-reproducible and therefore reinforced the aura of the unique artwork.

In such a reading, UbuWeb delivers the original yet unrealized promise of Maciunas' Fluxus Editions from the 1960s. Likewise, the Situationist servers—but also: every other electronic book, audio record, film, game copied and shared among people—provides the *Potlatch* that the Lettrist bulletin

7
Lippard 1973.

symbolized rather than realized. Digital technology, with its inherent facility of copying a file in infinite generations without quality loss and at comparatively negligible costs, would then have been the final missing building block for a working 'gift economy'. This idea had also influenced the first generation of net.artist in the 1990s, including Jodi, Heath Bunting, Alexei Shulgin, Vuk Ćosić and Olia Lialina, whose work mostly circulated outside exhibition spaces and suspended notions of 'the original'.

Concepts of a 'gift economy' based on 'the commons' did not only exist in the arts. They became generally popular with the Internet. By the 1990s, two popular phenomena substantiated them: Firstly, the GNU/Linux computer operating system, a fully working alternative to proprietary computer operating systems such as Unix, Windows and MacOS, programmed by volunteers and available for free downloading, copying and adaptation. Secondly, the popular culture of freely sharing music in the MP3 format through decentralized Internet services such as Napster. Kenneth Goldsmith, founder of UbuWeb, later described Napster as his 'epiphany':

> It was as if every record store, flea market and charity shop in the world had been connected by a searchable database and had flung their doors open, begging you to walk away with as much as you could carry for free. But it was even better, because the supply never exhausted; the coolest record you've ever dug up could now be shared with all your friends.[8]

Goldsmith 2015.

Linux received similar artistic appreciation, when in 1999, the Ars Electronica festival awarded it with its Golden Nica in the '.net' category, a prize meant for electronic media art. The jury cited Linux' cultural 'impact on the "real" world' as a reason for its decision, along with the intention 'to spark a discussion about whether a source code itself can be an artwork'.[9]

'Linux Torvalds Wins Prix Ars Electronica Golden Nica' 1999.

As if to prove that avant-garde art still does justice to its own name and historically runs ahead of popular culture, the fringe 'gift economy' concepts of Lettrists, Situationists and other counter-cultural groups became mass phenomena with Linux and MP3 file sharing three decades later. In his 1998 essay 'The Hi-Tech Gift Economy', British cultural studies scholar Richard Barbrook therefore called the Internet 'really existing anarcho-communism'. He credited the Situationist International as a forerunner but criticized that it 'could not escape from the elitist tradition of the avant-garde'.[10] For his references to Linux, Barbrook drew on the software developer Eric S. Raymond who, in the same year, had helped coin the term 'Open Source' for the new collaborative software development model. (Shortly after, 'Open Source' in software engineering became the blueprint for 'Open Access' in publishing.) In 2000, Raymond's paper *Homesteading the Noosphere* characterized the 'The Hacker Milieu as Gift Culture', arguing that 'Gift cultures are adaptations not to scarcity but to abundance'.[11] The promise of digital technology and the Internet was that electronic replication of digital zeros and ones had overcome the constraints and affordances of mechanical reproduction. In that light, Lippard's 'dematerialization' in conceptual art and Lyotard's postmodern 'immaterials' seemed to be issues that the digital commons had resolved.

As Aymeric Mansoux points out in his critical research on Open Source and its adoption in arts and culture, Raymond and others effectively paraphrased social-liberal economist John Maynard Keynes who, in 1930, had predicted that thanks to automation 'the *economic problem* may be solved … within one hundred years' so that an 'age of leisure' would follow.[12] Keynes' theory was influential in French post-war sociology and most prominently adopted by Guy Debord's teacher Henri Lefebvre. Debord and the Situationists expected a transformation of society into a leisure society, propagated machine-made 'industrial

10 Barbrook 2005.

11 Raymond 1998.

12 Keynes 1933 (2010). Mansoux' full doctoral research is still unpublished; an excerpt is available in Mansoux 2014.

painting' and based their 'Potlatch' on a firm expectation of the near end to economic scarcity.

In the late 1990s and early 2000s, the debate on the Internet as a gift economy found its most prominent voice in law professor Lawrence Lessig, who saw the technology as a means to a *Free Culture* outside traditional intellectual property and media industry regimes.[13] In 2001, Lessig co-founded the Creative Commons, a non-profit organization whose licenses encouraged people to apply the distribution principles of Open Source software such as Linux, including free copying and modification, to creative works of any kind, including texts, images and sound recordings. Wikipedia, founded in 2001, is among the best-known projects licensed under Creative Commons, and has become, besides Linux and MP3 file sharing, a poster case for the Internet as a 'digital commons'. Today, most academic Open Access publications are released under the terms of a Creative Commons License, too.

The underlying assumption is that in the age of digital media technology traditional copyright is too restricted for works to be truly publicly accessible, since it doesn't permit downloading or sharing. In former times, public access to a work of art, such as a sculpture, would be simply granted by the fact that it is physically accessible and visible to anyone because it is a piece of public property installed in a public space. Copyright would only restrict others from reproducing this work. Today, this no longer affects only commercial parties. Taking, for example, a cell phone picture of a public art work and sharing it online constitutes an act of reproduction and publishing (rather than legal personal use), thereby legally violating the artist's copyright.

When the World Wide Web and social media were still new, these issues were not seen as issues of access and shifts in consumption of culture, but rather as a paradigm shift in cultural production. This was perfectly in line with Maciunas' pre-Internet vision of art being 'obtainable by all and eventually produced by all'.[14] When legal scholar

Yochai Benkler coined the notion of 'commons-based peer production' in 2002,[15] he saw Wikipedia, Creative Commons and blogging as living proofs of a participatory 'Wealth of Networks', as opposed to traditional mass media with their sender/receiver and producer/consumer hierarchies.[16] On a larger economic scale, 'wealth of networks' implied that economic egoism would be overcome and would lead to more effective and sustainable production. Where Keynes saw automation as the key to overcome economic scarcity, Benkler advocated network collaboration.[17]

The latest Internet-cultural iteration of Benkler's optimism and, according to Mansoux,[18] of Keynes' 1930s post-scarcity visions is to be found in the so-called Maker movement. It was founded on the idea of using 3D printing and FabLabs for fully self-sufficient fabrication outside classical capitalist production and distribution chains. Bestseller writer and political consultant Jeremy Rifkin propagates a 'Third Industrial Revolution' based on these technologies. In his vision, they will lead to a 'Zero Marginal Cost Society'.[19] With nearly costless production, according to Rifkin, 'the Internet of Things, the collaborative commons' will lead to an 'eclipse of capitalism'.[20] In other words, Linux, MP3 file sharing and Wikipedia were seen as working commons because of their 'dematerialization'—with software and data being no longer subject to the material constraints of industrial production. But now this vision has transcended software and data to the point where even material products are expected to become shareable, like MP3 files. What Goldsmith had written about record stores 'begging you to walk away with as much as you could carry for free' with 'the supply never exhausted', would then apply to *any* store and *any* commodity.

From the 1990s to the early 2010s, these visions and debates remained largely exclusive to hacker culture, media activism and specialized areas of Internet art and media

15
Benkler 2006.

16
Ibid.

17
In 2008, the cultish 'Zeitgeist Movement' advocated a 'post-scarcity economy' in which economic and political decisions should be delegated to a central computer. Zeitgeist became a major force behind the Occupy protests in New York City and Frankfurt, Germany, both taking place at the center of the two cities' banking districts.

18
Mansoux 2014, see also note 12.

19
Rifkin 2014.

20
Ibid.; Rifkin 1996; Rifkin 2011.

theory. This changed only recently. In 2013, artist and filmmaker Hito Steyerl brought the issue to the centre of contemporary art when she coined the term 'circulationism' in an essay for the *e-flux journal*. Using filmmaking terminology, Steyerl stated that, in the Internet age, image production is superseded by 'postproduction'. She suggests:

> What the Soviet avant-garde of the twentieth century called productivism—the claim that art should enter production and the factory—could now be replaced by circulationism. Circulationism is not about the art of making an image, but of postproducing, launching, and accelerating it.[21]

The label 'circulationism' is not only a good fit for the endlessly 'post-produced' visual memes on image boards and moving image remixes on YouTube. The older Internet gift economies of Linux, Wikipedia, MP3 file sharing, UbuWeb and Situationist web sites are 'circulationist', too, since they are all sites of postproduction: Wikipedia with its policy not to publish any original research but only information from 'reputable sources', GNU/Linux as a clone of the Unix operating system that AT&T had developed in the 1970s. Steyerl concludes her essay with a Rifkin-esque extrapolation from software and data to hardware:

> Why not open-source water, energy, and Dom Pérignon champagne? If circulationism is to mean anything, it has to move into the world of offline distribution, of 3D dissemination of resources, of music, land, and inspiration.[22]

This view is shared in the contemporary philosophical movement of accelerationism. In their 2016 book *Inventing the Future: Postcapitalism and a World Without Work*, Nick Srnicek and Alex Williams, authors of the 2013 '#ACCELERATE MANIFESTO for an Accelerationist Politics',[23]

21
Steyerl 2013.

22
Ibid.

23
Srnicek and Williams 2013.

DOES THE TRAGEDY OF THE COMMONS REPEAT ITSELF AS A TRAGEDY OF THE PUBLIC DOMAIN?

advocate 'full automation' in combination with universal basic income.[24]

What is envisioned in these scenarios is the maximum expansion of the public domain through the abolition of work and any form of property.[25] Yet the political backgrounds of these writers and actors are extremely diverse, sometimes even contradictory: democratic socialist (Barbrook), neo-Leninist (Srnicek/Williams), right-wing libertarian (Raymond), liberal (Lessig), new age (Zeitgeist movement). On top of that, they range from contemporary art (Steyerl) to political consultancy of EU governments (Rifkin).

The Double Meaning of the 'Public Domain'

Strictly speaking, a gift economy, and a potlatch, can only exist if the difference between gift exchange and other forms of economic exchange is still in place. In a Keynesian full-automation, post-scarcity future, everything and hence nothing would be a gift. From the Lettrists to the 'Third Industrial Revolution', the gift thus covertly disappears from the scene. What's more, technology gradually replaces culture as agent and site of economic change. This results in artists' real-life public domain practices, from Lettrism to net.art and UbuWeb, being less and less acknowledged, even in the writings of artists such as Steyerl.

For their concept of the gift economy, Lettrists and Situationists drew on the French anthropologist Marcel Mauss (like Georges Bataille before and Jean Baudrillard after them). In the 1920s, Mauss had described the Potlatch as an 'archaic' economy of reciprocal gift exchange. Despite its common understanding as a counter-model to modern Western economic models of accumulation, the Potlatch ultimately is no less consumerist than modern capitalism, since it is based on social peer pressure of excessive giving and taking.[26]

In the contemporary art market, where 19th/20th century-style production and sales business models rule

24
Srnicek and Williams 2015.

25
A demand that Situationists and Anarchists had voiced much earlier, for example: Black 1986.

26
Mauss 1954.

and economic visions such as Rifkin's or Srnicek/Williams' are out of question, gift economies nevertheless remain a provocation. They squarely contradict the art market's principle of selling items to collectors and its creation of value through balancing an item's scarcity against collector demand. There could thus be no sharper contradiction than the one between a Potlatch, whether in its traditional or in its Lettrist form, and a contemporary art fair such as Art Basel or Frieze.[27]

Reformation-age pamphlets and graphic prints, including Dürer's, can be interpreted as early Western forms of an art in the public domain that circumvented traditional art markets (most of all, clerical and aristocratic patronage, churches and palaces). With early 20th century Dadaism as their precursor,[28] Situationism and Fluxus pioneered a practice of the public domain that transgressed the two realms of publishing media and public space. Merriam-Webster defines the public domain both as 'land owned directly by the government' and as 'the realm embracing property rights that belong to the community at large, are unprotected by copyright or patent'.[29] Contemporary English gravitates towards the second definition, the public domain as creative works that are free from individual rights claims. In other European languages, however, the double definition of 'the public domain' is still more pronounced, for example in the French expression 'domaine publique' and the Dutch 'publieke domein'. Legally, the concept thus refers to (a) physical property and (b) intellectual property: to physical territory that is not privately owned, and to creative work—writing, pictures, audiovisuals, designs, technical inventions—whose copyrights or patents have either expired or been given up.

The cybernetic utopia of circulationism, accelerationism, the Third Industrial Revolution, Open Source thus is to collapse both definitions and areas of the public domain into one: When the Dom Pérignon bottle

---

27
The dominance of the art market for early 21st century art—along with the political-economic shifts away from welfare state systems in Europe and elsewhere—means that even traditional forms of art in the public sphere are no longer firmly established. They no longer function as a Keynesian corrective to the free market. 1950s/60s Situationist psychogeography was a counter-movement to post-war modernist urbanism where drifting in the urban space contradicted any rigid, built structure. Yet today, even a classical modernist sculpture on a public square might qualify as 'situationist' when juxtaposed to an oligarch's private art depot locked away in an airport warehouse. See Segal 2012.

28
For example, the absurdist political leaflets and tabloids that were spread on streets and in parliament by the Berlin Dadaists.

29
Merriam-Webster 2016.

becomes infinitely downloadable, there is no more sense in differentiating physical from intellectual property. De jure, however, intellectual property has a clearly different status from physical property, being a metaphor born out of the invention of the printing press. Western jurisdictions put most intellectual property violations under civil law yet physical property violations under criminal law. 'Property' thus does not equal 'property'.

From Peer Production to Non-profit Organization

In 2012, *Forbes Magazine* estimated the total operating costs for the Internet at \$100-200 billion per year.[30] The figure only reflects operating costs of Internet service providers, excludes public investments into network infrastructure, costs for cell phone and telephone networks, expenses of Internet and media companies for maintaining their own services as well as computer hardware expenses of private households, public administrations, educational institutions et cetera. The Internet is not, to use Lyotard's word, an 'immaterial'. Optical fibre cables, its infrastructural backbone, are a degrading organic material that needs to be replaced every ten years. Scarcity of Internet resources may not be visible today since its infrastructure still benefits from massive private and public investment, and from slave labour combined with massively unfair trade in the production of electronic hardware. The current picture of data abundance might be skewed in the same way as the picture of electricity and oil abundance was skewed in the 1950s and 1960s.

With the world population projected to grow to ten billion people and more, global warming, depletion of natural resources, scarcity of energy, scarcity of raw materials needed for electronics and industrial production and, leaving hyperbolic prophecies aside, no realistic perspective that artificial intelligence robotics will soon make the bulk of manual labour obsolete (which would still beg the question

30
Price 2012.

on what energy and material resources those machines would run?), Keynes' hope that 'the *economic problem* may be solved' and create an age of leisure, appears dated. It is one of the contradictions of our present times that some of the same thinkers who subscribe to a philosophical 'new materialism'—with its focus on ecology, a 'parliament of things' (Latour), 'object-oriented ontology' and worries about the ecological catastrophe of the anthropocene—also believe in total leisure through total automation, as if computing and robotics operated in some immaterial void where the laws of physics, economy and natural resource exploitation are suspended.

Likewise, a critical look back at radical public domain projects of artists and media activists reveals countless flaws: The anti-copyright publishing of the Situationist International was only possible because the group was financed through gallery sales of paintings by its co-founding member Asger Jorn.[31] Fluxus' alternative business model of selling multiple editions faltered after less than a year. None of the participating artists followed the initial suggestion to sign over their individual copyright to Fluxus Editions.[32] Most Internet public domain projects were only possible through infrastructural support of public arts or educational institutions. UbuWeb, for example, runs on a university server in Mexico. Kenneth Goldsmith periodically warns users that the website might cease operation any day because of technical or legal difficulties, and recommends that people download its contents to their home computers. Unlike Fluxus Editions, UbuWeb does not have an economic compensation model for the artists whose works it provides, thus assuming that they have other sources of income (including the art market). The support infrastructures for Internet art in the public domain are, in the end, identical to those for traditional public art.

The most prominent digital commons projects have, in the meantime, become corporate. Linux started as a student project at a public university but is now financed by an IT industry consortium consisting, among others, of IBM, Intel, Samsung, Huawei, Oracle, Hewlett Packard, Qualcomm, Google, Facebook, Ebay, Toyota and Hitachi. In 2014, statistics showed that more than 80 per cent of Linux kernel code is currently written by corporate employees, with the mobile and embedded devices industry and its agenda driving the development of the software (among others, because Linux forms the basic software stack for micro controllers and for the Android smartphone operating system).[33] This does not change the fact that Linux is Open Source and freely available to anyone to download, use and modify. But ever since the Linux commons has become a corporate commons, it is evident that a commons does not necessarily need to be democratic; it is not necessarily a public domain under public governance.

Wikipedia and its sister project, the Wikimedia Commons, is subject to similar issues of governance and community representation. 90 per cent of Wikipedia's editors are male and most of them work in the technology industry. The non-profit organization running the encyclopaedia experiences major internal conflicts over organizational policy and transparency, and is being criticized for being 'increasingly run by those with Silicon Valley connections'.[34] Academic Open Access publishing has turned—squarely against its founders' intentions—into a revenue model for publishers that charge extra fees for giving up exclusive distribution rights.

Given their present state, none of these projects still fit the 1990s/2000s narratives of 'Anarcho-Communism' (Barbrook), 'bazaar' development (Raymond), 'read/write culture' versus 'read-only culture' (Lessig) and 'commons-based peer production' (Benkler). Instead, as a result of matured and professionalized organization, their ways of working have aligned themselves to those of industry consortia and design committees. It is difficult to spot organizational differences between non-profit Internet projects such as Linux,

Wikipedia and The Creative Commons, and the general sector of non-profit organizations, with their mix of volunteer and payroll work. The same questions that concern internal governance and external influence of non-profit, non-governmental organizations thus also concern the major Open Source and Open Content projects.

Tragedy of the Commons

Activist arts projects weren't free of these pressures and dynamics either. *Potlatch* ended up being reprinted as a book by Gallimard, France's most reputable publishing house. The book cover does not attribute it to the anonymous collective of the Lettrist International, but reads 'Guy Debord présente Potlatch (1954–1957)', with 'Guy Debord' typeset as the book's author's name. On page 7, the book bears the copyright mark '© Éditions Gallimard, 1996'.

When the ecologist Garrett Hardin coined term 'the commons' in 1968, he intrinsically linked it to the idea that they were doomed to fail in a 'tragedy'. In his paper, Hardin used the term in a way similar to the first dictionary definition of the 'public domain', namely as commonly used space.[35] However, he did not focus on the space as such but on its economic exploitation. For Hardin,

[35] Hardin 1968.

> The tragedy of the commons develops in this way. Picture a pasture open to all. It is to be expected that each herdsman will try to keep as many cattle as possible on the commons. ... As a rational being, each herdsman seeks to maximize his gain.[36]

[36] Ibid.

As a result, the herdsmen will have their cattle overgraze the shared resource:

> Each man is locked into a system that compels him to increase his herd without limit—in a world that is limited. Ruin is the destination toward which all men rush, each pursuing his own best interest in a society

DOES THE TRAGEDY OF THE COMMONS REPEAT
ITSELF AS A TRAGEDY OF THE PUBLIC DOMAIN?

that believes in the freedom of the commons. Freedom in a commons brings ruin to all.[37]

Today, Hardin's theory seem to be backed up by facts like the one that the world's biggest fifteen ships create as much environmental pollution as all the cars in the world because their engines run on waste oil, on open oceans.[38] Yet his notion of the commons has been criticized for lacking any differentiation between unregulated 'open access resources', such as open oceans, and policy-regulated 'common-pool resources', such as fisheries and forests, to use the terminology and examples of Nobel Prize-winning economist Elinor Ostrom.[39] Ostrom's notion of 'open access resources' must not be confused with 'open access' as in Open Access publishing. It concerns the exploitation of material resources while Open Access publishing is about the creation of immaterial goods. Furthermore, Ostrom's 'open access resources' are 'open' in the sense that their access and exploitation is completely unregulated, while Open Access publishing involves standards and rules for both, such as the provisions that an Open Access publication may not be commercially exploited or incorporated into a non-Open Access work.[40]

The various theories of the commons from Hardin to Ostrom indicate the lack of a generally agreed-upon concept of 'the commons' and thus, by implication, the lack of a universal notion of access. Terms such as 'Creative Commons' and 'Open Access' avoid these issues by offering practical solutions rather than theoretical definitions. Yet the issues remain unresolved. As the understanding and practice of copyright and intellectual property greatly differs across cultures and political systems (despite the Berne Convention for Protection of Literary and Artistic Works signed by all 170 United Nations member states), neither 'the commons', nor 'access' can be as universally defined as suggested for the Creative Commons and the Open Access movement.

[37] Ibid.

[38] Vidal 2009.

[39] Ostrom 2008.

[40] These are options in the Creative Commons Licenses, the licenses most frequently used for Open Access publications.

It is even questionable whether the notion of the commons applies to such a globally standardized system as the Internet. In its current status quo, the Internet can hardly be called a commons. It is, in Ostrom's terms, neither an open access resource nor a common-pool resource, because of the private ownership and control of most parts of its technical infrastructure. As it exists today, the Internet is also driven by industrial manufacturing of electronic hardware in low-wage countries, the inexpensive, ecologically questionable extraction of natural resources for manufacturing and electricity, and finally the concentration of Internet traffic and, increasingly, physical network infrastructure onto only a handful of large corporations (Google, Facebook, Amazon).

If one nevertheless suspends these objections and hypothetically assumes Benkler's belief that the Internet *is* a commons and that projects like Linux and Wikipedia constitute true commons production, then Hardin's 'tragedy of the commons' still provides a useful critical perspective. Increasingly, Linux and Wikipedia are exploited to serve as 'back-ends' for private services. Google's search engine now relies on Wikipedia for its top-ranked search results and uses the free encyclopaedia to auto-generate information summaries on search result pages themselves, thus encouraging users to remain on Google's advertising-financed site. By putting a proprietary service layer on top of Linux that, among others, heavily tracks user behaviour, Google's Android operating system effectively turns Linux into a proprietary operating system while legally conforming to its Open Source license. In a 2012 critical paper on Android, Kimberly Spreeuwenberg and Thomas Poell therefore conclude that the 'exploitation [of Open Source] has not only become more pervasive, but also more encompassing and multifaceted'.[41]

Hardin identifies economic growth and surplus extraction as the ultimate reason for the tragedy of the commons. This is just as true for a case such as Linux whose Open Source availability may be pessimistically

41
Spreeuwenberg and Poell 2012. There are more examples for the private-market exploitation of the Linux operating system, most prominently the use of Linux and other Open Source software as technical engines for running proprietary web services and social media. They have been left out here for the sake of brevity.

interpreted as a driver for surplus extraction like Google's—
which conversely results in wasteful gadget production and
resource consumption. Yet for Hardin, commons 'may work
reasonably satisfactorily for centuries' if there is no economic
growth and population numbers do not increase above 'the
carrying capacity of the land'. Gift economies, however, from
Potlatch to Kenneth Goldsmith's cornucopian record stores
and Hito Steyerl's open-sourced Dom Pérignon, *are* economies
of excess. They never pretended to be ecologically reasonable.
Against communist interpretations, Georges Bataille characterized the Potlatch as 'the meaningful form of luxury'
that 'determines the rank of the one who displays it'.[42]
The gift economies of Lettrism, Situationism, Fluxus,
1980s postpunk culture and later net.art involved excessive production of ephemera—pamphlets, multiples, performative leftovers, badges, pamphlets, code works—whose
exchange was poor people's luxury and whose volatility was
part of this 'circulationism'. In that sense, the tragedy of
the commons, violation of the commons' rules of constraint,
is a crucial part of these practices. 'Circulationism', if taken
as an umbrella term for everything from Berlin Dada to
UbuWeb, is not about ecological-ethical self-constraint, but
it amounts to a bohemian antithesis to scarcity, including
the artificially created scarcity of gallery art.

In this perspective, the Internet has only been a temporary accelerator (in the late 1990s and early 2000s perhaps
more than today) for a history that is politically, not techno-
logically driven. Being neither commons nor gift, the public
domain now exceeds separations of 'public space' and 'free
information', as these cultural practices and excesses show.

With thanks to Marcell Mars, Henry Warwick and Jens Schröter for their
suggestions and critical feedback.

[42] Bataille 1949 (1988), p. 76.

MISCOMMUNICATING PUBLICS

Barbara Neves Alves

There is a revolution of conversation occurring, and the people who always felt there was something wrong with the system are now coming together and talking about it. And that is huge.
—Tarif Ahmed[1]

One of the great rediscoveries of the past year has been the act of physically gathering on streets and squares—the transformation of the individual into a crowd, and more importantly into a 'public', and the collective assertion of protest creating an intense form of public visibility through the re-appropriation of public space.
—Eric Kluitenberg[2]

A Day 'Occupying' St. Paul's

On 15 October 2011, a Saturday morning, I headed to Paternoster Square in the heart of the City of London, excited about finally taking part in a chain of protests that had steadily emerged after the 'Arab Spring'[3] of December 2010. For months, the media had been collecting reports filled with strongly poetic imagery: power to the people, grassroots politics and a space to voice the opinion of those who feel excluded from the systems to which they are meant to contribute and belong. A certain nostalgia of left-wing activism informed and created a grassroots space in which to manifest frustration at the injustice of neo-liberal economic policies. The images of the time are powerful: transformed spaces, self-organized micro-communities, a lively online network of support and thousands of individual voices visible in online posts, in photos, in signs and paintings held by anonymous crowds. There were writers, academics, activists, artists, celebrities, politicians, all affected by and affecting this chain of events—participating in a wide variety of discourses surrounding the occupation of a city square. In occupying public space, a movement emerged and rapidly spread, giving visibility to 'the 99%'.[4]

BEING PUBLIC

Arriving at St. Paul's Cathedral, I realized that the police had cut off the entrance to Paternoster Square, the meeting point for the 'occupation'. Handmade posters were spread across the ground and people were standing in small crowds, under heavy police surveillance, sipping coffee and chatting at the Cathedral steps. After a while, the chatter became more purposeful: 'Occupy London' would settle in front of St Paul's Cathedral. A landing on the staircase that leads up to St. Paul's entrance was cleared, creating a stage from which to address the crowd: *'Mic check, mic check!'* was repeated from the first line of the crowd to the last—forming the human amplification that made up for the lack of electricity. *The people's microphone* was in place, resonating to and with the crowd.

The first intervention was on communication. Someone first explained that it was better not to clap, to avoid constant interruptions; and then how to communicate by outlaying a choreography of gestures signalling (for example):[5]

—'agreement': hands shaking in the air;

—'disagreement': hands shaking towards the ground;

—'interruption due to any technical issue': hands in a perpendicular position.

The word *consensus* started punctuating every intervention, a constant reminder that we were gathered to create an Occupy London that belonged to us all.

Sitting on the floor, amidst the crowd, I repeated what was said. It was exciting and emotional to be surrounded by other people, to shout out words and to hear the shouting next to me. Being part of the 'people's mic' (as the people's microphone was referred to at Occupy) lent physicality to listening—it gave us the feeling of strength through uniformity, a collective in the act of communicating—and it was deeply moving.

Gradually, this general assembly shaped an agenda for the day: first, we would divide into groups and propose

---

4 An expression that constitutes a widespread Occupy slogan, originating from a flyer distributed at a NYC General Assembly in August 2011: 'Occupy Wall Street is a leaderless resistance movement with people of many colors, genders and political persuasions. The one thing we all have in common is that We Are The 99% that will no longer tolerate the greed and corruption of the 1%. We are using the revolutionary Arab Spring tactic to achieve our ends and encourage the use of nonviolence to maximize the safety of all participants'. `http://occupywallst.org/`.

5 For more information on the hand signals used see Batista #searchunderoccupy.

topics for discussion. Each group would have a spokesperson and three minutes to present their topics for the crowd to vote on. Then, all those present would work in smaller groups focused on specific topics. Each smaller group was composed of around twenty people and was given around twenty minutes to work on their topic. In the group I was part of, people were engaging and enthusiastic, but the time frame and the number of people restricted the space for discussion. Gradually, it became obvious that we had 'assembly experts' among us, who led 'conversations'. Among the topics proposed: arranging for water, food and sanitation; managing a dialogue with the authorities; teaching the crowd what to do 'when' the police eventually charged; talking to the priest at St. Paul's—all practical matters stressing the logistical aspects of occupation.

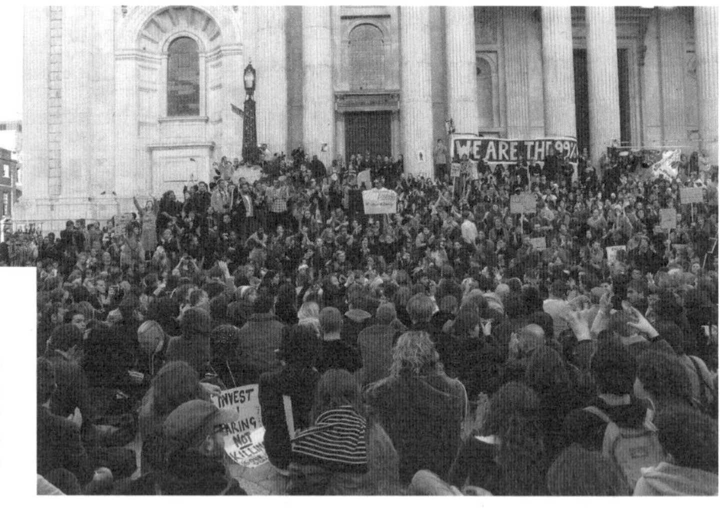

Protesters in front of St. Paul's Cathedral, London, United Kingdom, 15 October 2011. Photo by Crispin Semmens, 2011, courtesy Crispin Semmens, Creative Commons, licensed under CC-BY-SA 2.0.

Three hours later, we were divided into groups, surrounded by hundreds of police, horses, dogs and vans. Cut off from the rest of the city, we could hear a distant sound of protest from the many that were denied entrance to the square. Each group was now responsible for implementing the topics agreed upon in the general assembly. I started moving from group to group:

BEING PUBLIC

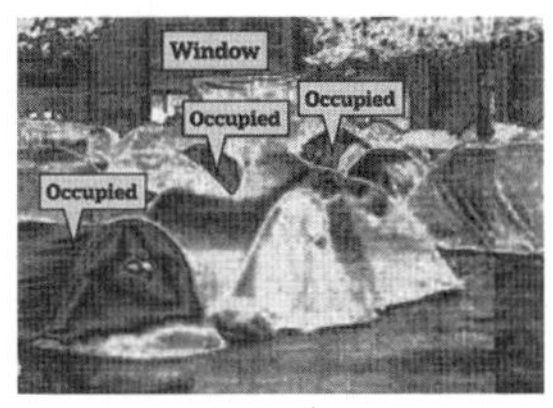

Thermal image of the London Occupy camp, and part of a set of images taken by an independent thermal imaging company (commissioned by the *Daily Mail*), October 2011. In the original image most of the tents are depicted in magenta, while the tents marked with 'occupied' present a distinct colour range (blue, green, yellow, red). From: Tom Kelly and Damien Gayle 'The thermal images that prove 90% of tents in the Occupy camp in London are left EMPTY overnight,' published by MailOnline, 26 October 2011.

6
A growing feeling of claustrophobia as well as a fear of the police made me realize that Occupy was not important enough (to me) to justify the sacrifices it might demand. I managed to cut through the police line, but stayed nearby for hours, observing.

7
We instantly became kettled by the police. For information on kettling see for example, Netpol, 'Guide to "Kettles"', https://netpol.org.

O.K. we've ordered public toilets. They will be arriving soon, so we can inform the police spokesperson that there is no longer an issue there.

We'll set up a kitchen in that corner. We need protection against the rain and a place to store donated food and kitchenware.

I have just contacted the lawyer. We should ask everyone to write his phone number on their body and give no information to the police when arrested. No one talks! No names!

I was surprised by the incredible 'practicality' of what was happening: ordering toilets? Who's paying for this? Lawyers? Kitchenware? Suddenly I felt disoriented. Where was the spontaneity I had imagined from such an assembling of people? The process suddenly seemed premeditated and prepared. People brought tents, but also tables and brooms, infrastructure, spokespeople, lawyers and funding. Occupy 'experts' from Spain were present to support setting up. It became apparent that many of these 'consensual' decisions had been carefully and strategically planned. I felt as if I were part of a pantomime in which, like a biddable audience, I played my role by waving hands.

As night fell, more and more armed police arrived, tightening their circle around the protesters;[6] Brazilian drums and dancing started echoing along with shouts of 'Do not fight back!', 'We are a peaceful movement!' The familial, playful vibe gave way to a growing tension between police and 'occupiers', as the police surrounded a now much smaller group of them. No more interventions or discussions, the only shouting was words of advice regarding how to behave towards the police 'kettling'.[7] As diplomatic efforts failed to grant an occupied space, it seemed to me that an awareness on how mediated the

MISCOMMUNICATING PUBLICS

acts of both occupiers and police were, held the line within each side, everyone conscious of constant uploads on Twitter, Facebook and Occupy-related blogs, as well as of the presence of many reporters from broadcast media.

Around ten o'clock at night, tired and cold, heading home I saw dozens of police vans and horses parked on the side roads to St. Paul's ready to be mobilized. This was a disproportionate display of strength, but explicit violence would not be used to clean the square, perhaps due to the strong mediatization of the events. I was sad. The poetic images in which I placed faith had been replaced by disappointment. Occupy did not create the free-flowing space for a politics of the people that I had imagined. Quite the opposite, I was surprised about the role communication played in drawing a consensus that, in fact, limited participation and seemed to equalize the plural dimensions of our being there.

Communication devices employed by Occupy—such as the general assembly and people's mic—stressed consensus in order to project a movement, but overlooked the political dimension outlined by the many miscommunications emerging from occupation. In this text, I propose a productive sense of miscommunication that layers consensus with the possibility of other political formations that draw a more diverse perspective of the publics affected by occupy and broaden what it means to participate in communicative arenas.

Introducing Miscommunication and Faithful Communication

The presumption that there is an ease of exchange between subjects—defined in generic terms—is a common practice in the field of communication design, but it prevents us from further querying the conditions, contexts and publics of an exchange. Because in counting on a general 'good sense' of how things are understood, communication design is, in fact, taking on a set of assumptions that affect the quality of participation in a communicative arena, flattened to the conditions in which communication design assumes an agreement around the terms of an exchange.

I propose to use and adapt Stengers' term, 'faithful communication',[8] to designate a communication process oriented toward addressing a public in a way that is seen to be unaltered by the designer, context or medium in which communication takes place. The idea of faithful communication involves processes of communication constructed upon formulations of the public that are inclusive in the sense that communication is set out in terms that might be generally understood, by working a space of common representations. But these common representations reinforce and reproduce consensual understandings of the public without misunderstanding,[9] which frame communication as a space of rational, discursive interchange. This space of exchange and negotiation rests on common terms and is at the foundation of political models of communication constructed from representation. It accounts, for example, for the public sphere of deliberative democracy and notions of the public rooted in the idea of faithful communication. It is an idealized view of faithful communication—one ignoring misunderstanding—that allows, for example, for a prevailing metaphor of the public within representative democracy: an image of a body constituted by the sum of many bodies[10] as an illustration of a public equally represented within modes of government and capable of communicating to exchange ideas over common affairs.

In this text I take a close look at Occupy's communication devices to propose miscommunication as a productive part of communication design. In exploring miscommunication, I am not looking to observe the ways in which 'good', frictionless communication unfolds, but rather to the ways in which miscommunication might be seen to be more characteristic of communicative exchanges, and allow for different political formations and a broader sense of the public in designing communication. In this way I am proposing

8
Stengers 2005, p. 189.

9
As Stengers writes in ibid.: 'And the practical certainty of misunderstanding is something an ecology of practice has to affirm without nostalgia for what would be faithful communication.'

10
See for example: Abraham Bosses' illustration on the front cover of *Leviathan* by Thomas Hobbes in 1651, British Library, 'Collection Items', www.bl.uk.

MISCOMMUNICATING PUBLICS

miscommunication as a concept and practice to query the position of the designer in a communicative setting.

Miscommunication is part of communication, but one that troubles, challenges faithful communication. It is not about misunderstanding emerging around shared representations, but rather about different inhabitations of a communicative situation that are not restricted to representational frames. Miscommunication is what is overlooked within the generic terms set out by 'good communication'. Because miscommunication happens in dynamic moments of transition, of a fissure in 'good communication', contingent to the particular grounds in which a communicative exchange takes place. These particular grounds challenge the position of a neutral, or distant mediator, to a view on mediation as an interfering and contributing factor in communication. In this sense, miscommunication is a way to work pass preconditioned readings of participants, situations and problems, shifting attention to what may be disruptive, puzzling, dismissed or troublesome within a communicative setting.

The 'practical certainty of misunderstanding' means faithful communication is an ideation, and in this text I move away from idealized constructs of the public by proposing the figure of the idiot as a figure of miscommunication, to explore that which takes place or emerges from outside the terms of faithful communication. 'The idiot' is proposed by Isabelle Stengers in 'The Cosmopolitical Proposal'[11] to slow down reasoning and allow other perspectives to help us think about a situation. I transport the figure of the idiot to the field of communication design by working the idiot as a figure of miscommunication that queries how a consensus brought by faithful communication overrides a multitude of qualities of participation. While apparently complying to the terms of faithful communication, the idiot in fact inhabits communication differently and provokes impasses to 'good communication', brought by miscommunication. These impasses may draw

11
Stengers 2005b.

possibilities to rethink the terms of participation in communicative arenas—open to new partakers, connections and exchanges.

The Idiot as a Figure of Miscommunication

Stengers develops the character of the idiot from Deleuze and Guattari[12] as

> the one who always slows the others down ... [by] resist[ing] the consensual way in which the situation is presented and in which emergencies mobilize thought or action. ... because 'there is something more important'.[13]

The resistance produced by the idiot stems from a different perspective that seems to paralyze any 'normal' relationship of address or common views on a subject: 'Don't ask him why; the Idiot will neither reply nor discuss the issue. The Idiot is a presence or, as Whitehead would have put it, produces an interstice.' In the openness brought about by such a response, the idiot creates a space that Stengers proposes as a state of indeterminacy. As she explains:

> And it happens in the mode of indeterminacy, that is, of the event from which nothing follows, no 'and so...' but that confronts everyone with the question of how they will inherit from it.[14]

This state of indeterminacy originates from a very particular type of fissure in the terms of an exchange.[15] In terms of communication, the state of indeterminacy produced by the idiot creates a productive form of miscommunication that signals to a view that is parallel, other, unaccounted for. In this sense exposing the situation to unknown perspectives because: '... the idiot demands that we slow down, that we don't consider ourselves authorized to believe we possess the meaning of what we know'.[16] A state of inde-

12
Deleuze and Guattari 2009.

13
Stengers 2005b, p. 994.

14
Ibid., p. 996.

15
Ibid., p. 994–95.

16
Ibid.

terminacy produced by the idiot's miscommunication is not to be resolved; rather, one can dismiss its occurrence—reassured by the terms of faithful communication—or position oneself, affected by indeterminacy. In this sense, the miscommunication produced by the idiot may generate discrepancies between general arguments and practical grounds where communication productively opens up space to witnessing and connecting potentially hidden, different qualities of participation.

A good example of the idiot producing miscommunication in a communication process working to achieve agreement and consensus can be found in the example of Occupy because those taking part in Occupy manifestly believed in participating in a set of procedures to arrive at a better situation. Nevertheless, instances of miscommunication permeate these processes, pointing to other dimensions of the political surrounding Occupy. I will look into two particular examples: the general assembly and people's mic.

The General Assembly and People's Mic

Within Occupy, modes of political resistance encouraged clear forms of communication: in occupying a pre-occupied space,[17] in managing the logistics of a long-term protest,[18] and in disseminating a movement.[19] Communication devices assumed a double value, logistic and symbolic, reinforcing the imagery of occupation—like the crowd, the handwritten protest sign, the Guy Fawkes mask, or the tent camp.[20] In employing these devices, Occupy focused on establishing the ideological and strategic value of agreement of projecting a consensus. It was important to create a public capable of resisting authority, but also of organizing a movement and Occupy relied on the general assembly and the people's mic as communication devices to accomplish this.

The general assembly (GA) is a decision-making gathering, open to all. Topics are proposed, discussed and

17
Hartcourt 2012.

18
Taussig 2012.

19
Mitchell 2012.

20
'... one might single out the image of the tent and the encampment, the sign that these were not temporary or transitory gatherings like the typical political rally but manifestations of a long term resolve'. Ibid., p. 14.

voted upon as a form of direct democracy, with the purpose of achieving consensus. At Occupy London, GAs allowed three-minute presentations, which were necessarily cut into small sentences that could be easily repeated by the people's mic. This constrain led to half of each presentation becoming an echo of itself. The response to these presentations could take three forms: signing-up to address the crowd through the GA, expressing agreement/disagreement through hand gestures or participating in smaller group discussions.

The conditions to participate in GAs were established *a priori* with the aim of generating a space of 'good' communication by consensus; a consensus that equalized all voices into one, allowing the movement to project a united front. But these conditions also restricted the staging of communication, as Bernard E. Hartcourt recalls in relation to Occupy Chicago:

> … a protester began challenging one of the speakers, … repeatedly interrupting the conversation, breaking the order of 'stack'. The other protesters started by asking him to respect the process and to put himself on stack. He continued to heckle the speaker. … There was enforcement brought to bear on the disorderly protester. He was excluded from the gathering. The conversation resumed.[21]

Hartcourt's description illustrates how consensus can be confined to those agreeing to the rules of communication already set in place. But also how communication manifestly assumes a role in threading notions of political value—agreement or disagreement—around the formation of publics.

The stress on consensus—that nothing is done without everyone's consent—stems from a strong affinity between Occupy and the anarchist tradition[22] that aims to contest political systems based on representativity with the idea of a direct democracy that opens the

[21] Hartcourt 2012, pp. 42–43.

[22] David Graeber refers to four points shared between Occupy and aanarchist principles: first, the refusal to grant legitimacy to existing political institutions, thus refusal to issue demands; second, a refusal to accept the legitimacy of the existing political order, thus occupying space according to a moral order and not a legal one; third, a refusal to create an internal hierarchy and deciding to take on forms of consensus based on direct democracy; finally, the 'embrace of prefigurative politics' camps as space of experiment to creating institutions to a new society. Here Graeber gives the example of general assemblies, kitchens, clinics, media centres operating on anarchist principles of mutual aid and self-organization. Graeber 2012.

possibility of all being heard and involved in political action. In fact, what was being communicated within the confines of the square contrasted with what was being communicated outside: inside there was a clear network of specialists running the occupation; from the outside, the occupation seemed to result from the pure leaderless concern of the collective.

The GA not only aimed for consensus, but also put forth the idea of direct democracy and absence of leaders as counter to representative democracy: there is no one representing the people but themselves. This outlines a strong symbol, the 'common grounds' intensely explored within the media at the time:

> The park is where protesters' grievances overlap. It's literally common ground. … The governing process they choose is itself a bedrock message of the protest. … on the ground is where the protesters are building an architecture of consciousness.[23]

The fact that the Occupy movement aimed at being leaderless, and non-representable, signalled the importance of mediation and communication as both a practical tool and an ideological symbol. In transforming into a symbol of Occupy, the GA allowed for one of the main marks of the Occupy movement, the absence of claims: 'As soon as someone proposes something—one proposes vocabulary, an ideology, which can only have effects of domination.'[24] However, the conditions of production of discourse were not questioned.

Communication devices such as the GA and people's mic seem to have left the issue of leadership open enough for those with their own agenda to influence people gathered in protest. For the people who arrived without plans, it was a space of vulnerability. Again, participation also depended on the personality of those involved, due to how the space itself was organized. For example for those unwilling, or too

23
Kimmelman 2011, p. 7.

24
Hartcourt 2012, p. 39.

BEING PUBLIC

shy, to step up on a stage and face the crowd and speak, participation was severely reduced to mostly a waving of hands, which relegated them to a position where they would have apparently nothing to say. Furthermore, this waving of hands actually left little place to signal disagreement, either because one felt group pressure, or because shaking arms with hands pointing towards the ground is not visible within a crowd. This added a layer of miscommunication that did not emerge around a discursive exchange, but around performative dimensions of communication.

Miscommunications also became apparent in the people's mic. When setting up GAs, Occupy was forbidden by the authorities to use electrical amplifiers, loudspeakers or megaphones, which very much limited large-scale communication. Working around the prohibition, voices were amplified through a 'human microphone': the audience repeated the speech of a speaker, sentence by sentence, by sections of the audience—from the front to the back—in order to communicate the speech to the whole of the crowd, as in an echo.

The need to speak in heavily truncated sentences—to enable repetition—lends itself to communication that becomes generic, emotional or technical in nature, but nonetheless encourages feelings of deep engagement as each person is simultaneously listening and speaking, creating the sensation of active participation. Attention is divided, not focusing primarily on content, but on a bodily participation, which adds a strong performative dimension to communication. People do not ponder whether they *will* repeat before repeating, they do so because of the affective principle of 'united together' for a 'common cause'. The space between hearing and saying allows no time for analysis, reflection or dissent. Instead, the crowd functions as an echo chamber—even when shaping an emotional experience.

On 16 November 2011, within 'Occupy Wall Street' in New York, writer Arundhati Roy gave a speech at the 'People's University' at Judson Memorial Church in Washington Square

25

A video of Roy's inter-
vention is available at
Roy Groupies, *Arundhati
Roy @ the People's Uni-
versity*, YouTube,
17 November 2011.

26

Recently, the people's mic
is being used as a form of
contestation within uni-
versity campuses in the
U.S. as a means to dis-
rupt public presentations
deemed as conservative. In
these cases, the people's
mic disrupts speeches by
amplifying an intervention
from a member of the audience to interrupt speakers.
Other times, speeches are
disrupted by being repeated
by the audience, subvert-
ing both conventions: the
individual speech and the
human microphone. See
Rey 2012. During Occupy
Wall Street, it was even
employed as a tactic by
the police in an attempt to
reason with occupiers. See
Taussig 2012, p. 82.

27

Ibid., p. 83.

Park.[25] The first part of her speech constituted a slow and emotional collective reading as each sentence was broken into small parts, repeated and amplified by the people's mic. However, in the second part, Roy addressed her audience with ease as she answered questions from the crowd with no amplification present, or necessary. The people's mic had become a formality, an identifying trace, a kind of communication ritual.[26]

As a tactic used to circumscribe a technical limitation and defy the authorities, this human mode of amplification makes a strong statement. As imagery of occupation, it holds powerful symbolic value: all are speaking, united. As a ritual and performance, it keeps us active as participants—'in repetition you come to grips with trauma'.[27] The strength of the people's mic is not in communicating effectively, but in mobilizing affective dimensions that surpass a staging of 'good communication'. As a symbol of unity, the people's mic generates miscommunications by amplifying not only to increase volume, but adding to the performativity of communication.

Miscommunication arises within the paradox of the practical sense of repeating to amplify, now transformed into a formality, a symbol, where echoing actually disturbs faithful communication as it creates an impasse, a delay, disconnecting speaking from listening and, in this sense, opening a space to other modes of engaging in communication. I see an opportunity to rethink communication as a site where different political possibilities might emerge, by working from forms of miscommunication that remained unaddressed by Occupy.

Occupy and Miscommunication

During occupation, the weeks of occupying, and the ideological movement of Occupy, there were several instances of ambiguity, irony, contradiction, contrast, paradox, and nonsense. Much of these had as pre-condition Occupy's principle of refusal: refusal of a pre-occupation, of political models tied to neo-liberalism, refusal of leadership, refusal of representation, refusal of claims, refusal to move. It was as if all meanings could be occupied, overruled, made personal, and at the same time multiple and part of a multitude. The point was not to seize power but to manifest the power of refusal. As Mitchell proposes, there was refusal 'to make specific demands whilst creating a space in which multiple demands can be made'.[28] In this sense, Occupy became a common place for innumerable contradictions: interpolating the whole world, each and every subject, but also abstract concepts, like the motto 'occupy everything'[29] indicates. The openness of this space seemed to work as an echo chamber of its own force and contrasted with the consensus emerging from the GA.

In terms of communication, Occupy focused on becoming representative yet engaged with the practicalities of occupying. Miscommunications proliferate in the spaces between these dimensions: between the idea of the GA as a space producing a consensus and the manipulation of Occupy's agenda observed above; in the symbolic gestures allowing for all to take part, while only agreement was to be visible to the crowd; in how the ideology of equal participation in the oratory of the GA contrasts with how space was designed to speak from an elevated stage facing the crowd; in the symbolic strength of one voice with no demands against a proliferation of posters held up by protesters and numerous statements online, that made visible multiple demands; in the people's mic being a practical solution of repeating to be heard, whilst leaving little space for actual listening; or the fact that the people's mic became a symbol of speech that compromises speech by breaking it into repeatable sentences; in how a practical tactic transforms into a symbol; and in participating in-between the representative and performative.

The practical dimensions that disappointed me at St. Paul's become interesting grounds to explore in this context, because miscommunication points to other formations of publics, beyond ideological ones, and to different types of

28
Mitchell 2012, p. 10–11.

29
'Occupy would ultimately seize even abstract, conceptual objects as well: Time, Theory, the Disciplines, the Arts, the Imagination, the Media, the US. A poster with the words "Occupy Everything" spelled out the unlimited scope of this figure', in ibid.

communicative arenas. It seems the domain of the practical, the grounds upon which processes of communication were occurring, allowed miscommunication to permeate communication and generate a sense of paradox, of idiocy which, if acknowledged, creates impasses to faithful communication that demands a positioning that may reshape the terms on which communication is designed.

We use our magic to thwart their magic. They have pepper spray. We have burning sage. They prohibit microphones. We have the people's microphone. They prohibit tents. We improvise tents that are not tents but what nomads used before North Face. They build buildings higher than Egyptian pyramids, but that allows our drumming to reverberate all the louder and our projections of images and emails at night to be all the more visible and magical.[30]

30
Taussig 2012, p. 77.

Grounding Miscommunication

As occupation required 'structure—general assemblies, websites, Twitter accounts, UPS deliveries, teach-ins, libraries, medical units and volunteer lawyers'[31] an intense logistical operation took place, aimed primarily at establishing its territory, its grounds. However, to structure meant more than building practical infrastructure. It meant that materialities were also bodies projecting their own set of disputes. Actions staged political resistances in unforeseen ways: walking, standing, shouting, rubbing shoulders, moving things, holding posters, and posters embodied as masks.[32] For example, when authorities prohibited gasoline-powered generators at Zucotti Park in New York City, people pedalled fixed bicycles to generate electricity, doubling the reading of bikes: now fixed in place while staging a resistance.

31
Hartcourt 2012, p. 43.

32
Taussig 2012, p. 9.

Occupy rendered the physical *act* of occupation as a generic figure to set a political *movement* in place: different sites adopted similar guidelines during occupation in order to identify themselves as part of the larger Occupy movement.[33] Each site could have allowed for miscom-

33
See for example: OCCY-
PYLSX 2011.

                                          BEING PUBLIC

munications emerging from specific challenges, groups of people and locations, to create political disputes around each occupation. Moreover, the pairing of *act/movement* relocated into other dichotomies such as *space/cause, particular/universal*, triggering ambiguities that weakened Occupy as a political movement.

The radicalism and the political potential that could emerge from looking at the particulars of each site being occupied were denied in favour of construing a movement. For example, politicians tried to attack the Occupy camp as dirty, propelling the idea that the camp lacked hygiene—a health and safety hazard—and that the camp was polluting and destroying the space of a wider public than the protesters. Cleaning was not only used as a metaphor for the idea that the space needed to be cleaned from occupation, it was also an act as political as occupying itself. Since authorities used the argument of cleaning to de/re-occupy the square, occupiers took matters into their own hands and started cleaning. As occupiers tackled the health and safety requirements of the municipality it became obvious that the dichotomy dirty/clean referred to other dimensions. In accusing Occupy of dirtiness, the movement, and not the camp, was under attack. I assume that, in concentrating on the 'occupying act', on occupation per se as the grounds for a political movement, perhaps Occupy could have moved this discussion to a political dimension, but cleaning was displaced to the generic space of an Occupy movement, in this sense neutralizing its political potential.

Had Occupy been centred on the act of occupying (how/what to Occupy) rather than on projecting a consensual stage around occupation, the intense discussion of logistics would have made sense. However, by insisting on generalizing, discussions around occupation become generic across different cities, and Occupy played into the hands of its opponents. In criticizing the events at a square, opponents of Occupy criticized the act to weaken the movement. A focus on the act of occupying could have led to disputes around the particular grounds of each occupation. Disputes that could have allowed for productive miscommunications to play out on the level of the materialities.

An example of such a materiality was the tent. Occupying took full form in the act of sleeping on the square, transformed into a camp, covered with tents. This was not a temporary demonstration[34] but a durational protest. However, while the tent became a sign of permanence—even if no strings were attached to the ground—the tent in itself is a sign of nomadism. So, when captured as symbol of Occupy, the tent transposed this contrast between its role as a sign of permanence and transience.

At a certain point, the camp in London became the focus of a dispute among critics of Occupy who claimed that the tents were empty as occupiers went back to the comfort of their homes. Other rumours started being associated with the tent camp: that it was unsafe, that there once was a rape, or that the distribution of tents in the campus was simply re-enacting the pre-existing differences of wealth among the collective of protesters.[35]

At St. Paul's, the strongest rumour was that the tents were empty. Media reports alleged that tents had been photographed with thermal lenses, suggesting vacant tents.[36] A debate between reporters, experts in thermal imaging and protesters discussed the reliability of these tests and the 'reality' of occupation in the media. This revealed key aspects of the tent as a symbol for Occupy. The tent is configured as a singular space of privacy in the open publicness of the occupied square. The thin cloth of the tents was the dividing line between public and private spaces and, as any private space, its interior was concealed. But the fact that this space was 'open' in such a public space bore striking contrast and constituted the ultimate provocation. The tent became a surface of projections of what was unseen, invisible: the tents sheltered secret meetings, fugitives, drugs and, symbolically, the very absence of protesters. This indeterminacy opened up a

34
Mitchell 2012, p. 14.

35
'As time goes by—horror of horrors!—something like property and real estate interests surface. Someone quips that there is an Upper East Side section of tents in the park, and one hears muttering of gentrification as if this utopic space is reproducing what it is against.' In Taussig 2012, p. 63.

36
Thermal images of Occupy camp in London, taken by an independent thermal imaging company and commissioned by the *Daily Mail.*

significant sense of emptiness that conjures a sort of zero degree of representation, and reveals the paradoxes of opening invisible private spaces inside public spaces.

Inhabiting Indeterminacy

The example of the tent sets out modes of inhabiting the political that transport communication to the territory of the practical where the stress is not in interlocution, and communication is not subject to achieving forms of agreement or disagreement. In 'Experimenting with Refrains: Subjectivity and the Challenge of Escaping Modern Dualism', Stengers expresses this different sense of the political, where what is at stake is not common values, but rather the fostering of a set of connections. Connections that allow 'hesitat[ing] about our conditions of thought',[37] in this sense creating new readings, brought from being connected and affected by a situation, where one 'do[es] not think in terms of determination but in terms of entangling speculative questions'.[38]

Occupy is an attempt to occupy, to claim a territory, but it is a territory where assertions are undermined by what is happening in public space. This creates miscommunications that can be productive of impasses—of indeterminacy—at those key junctures of saying how we should live in a democratic space, and based on what kind of exchanges. In proposing the idiot as a conceptual character, Stengers is asking her readers to occupy places of indeterminacy, as a practical proposition to inhabit and think the political:

> And this means reclaiming an ecology that gives the situations we confront the power to have us thinking feeling, imagining, and not theorizing about them. In this I am a Marxist—the point is to 'change the world, not to understand it', but I add that this implies giving to the world the power to change us, to 'force' our thinking.[39]

[37] Stengers 2008, p. 41.

[38] Ibid., p. 48.

[39] Ibid., p. 57.

In Occupy, the participatory processes devised were constructed from the experience of anarchist movements, which in their drive to become consensual ignored miscommunications. These miscommunications in turn present an opportunity for new political configurations to emerge. Miscommunications, which were often not discursive but manifested themselves as impasses to occupation, interrupting ideas of faithful communication, calling on other ways of being affected by Occupy and presenting an opportunity for new political questions to emerge.

Moments of idiocy, states of indeterminacy, as described by Stengers, are states that have both infinite potential and definitive impossibility. The idiot, in provoking states of indeterminacy, shapes disturbances that work communication into productive forms of miscommunication where '… we don't consider ourselves authorized to believe we possess the meaning of what we know'.[40] A miscommunication by idiocy transports the practical into communication, and challenges the terms of faithful communication.

Stengers appropriates Deleuze and Guattari's 'idiot' as a character indicating a paradoxical state, which provokes an indeterminacy of senses. This paradoxical state creates an openness to indeterminacy that matters when considering miscommunication within the field of communication design. First, because it draws in matters of positioning and affect, which contemplate an attachment[41] and positioning that involves a 'thinking with', and being implicated with what will happen in the realm of a practice. Choosing to work from indeterminacy implies allowing the nonsense of the idiot to resonate in design processes and the personal commitment to allow indeterminacy to provoke political questions. Secondly, because indeterminacy calls on a performative quality where miscommunication links diverse perspectives, even if incapable or unwilling of interlocution; moving from representational frames to consider materialities and affects in communication. Finally, indeterminacy demands

40
Stengers 2005b,
pp. 994–95.

41
Puig de la Bellacasa 2011.

a political transformation from inhabiting a situation, while lacking keys to interpret or unlock it.

In terms of communication design this means that the positioning of the designer matters and that the concern of the designer as mediator is not in threading questions of accountability or public visibility but rather an affected and speculative inhabiting of a communicative situation where miscommunication surpasses the level of what might or might not be equally understood.

In emphasizing the value of faithful communication, the design of communication limits the conditions for participation to the sharing of a common knowledge of political problems, based upon political spaces that allow for interlocution, but that render affect silent and exclude miscommunication *a priori* as condition to participate. In engaging with Occupy I have attempted to demonstrate how it becomes interesting to probe what it means when people try to work through processes to arrive at consensus, but are also producing miscommunication and modes of indeterminacy that re-root the pursuit of the good, of the faithful, to allow for other forms of political participation.

The question becomes one of understanding communication design in a way that allows for a more complex and eco-positioned discussion of political matters, and shaping of political arenas, where what is at stake is '… a matter of imbuing political voices with the feeling that they do not master the situation they discuss, that the political arena is peopled with shadows of that which does not have a political voice, cannot have or does not want to have one'.[42] Thus, not narrowing participation to those capable or willing to enter processes of interlocution.

The idiot as a figure of miscommunication shapes connections that suspend what would be assumed as logical correspondences, and allows other layers, other connections, to surface. Indeterminacy renders miscommunication visible by transporting exchanges from the domain of the representative to a practical dimension and by drawing other modes

42
Stengers 2005b,
pp. 995–96.

of participation that are not shaped around representation, but rather a 'lived' dimension of communication.

Conclusion

My expectations when participating in Occupy were that we would be tentatively shaping an occupation and in doing so addressing how and what it meant to take over public space. At St. Paul's I felt that my presence was rendered as somewhat idiotic, leaving me with a set of questions about how a diversity of publics and multiple modes of assembly could be brought into a political space. In this text, I expanded on these questions by exploring the idiot as a figure of miscommunication, but still questions remain as to probing communication design from the position of the idiot. For example, at the site of Occupy, what could working from the position of the idiot in the terrain imply? I consider that transporting communication to practical grounds allows other terms for participation in shaping a grassroots movement such as Occupy. But my reaction to falling into the script of how to assemble was to redraw from Occupy. My idiotic presence did not create an impasse to communication, but rather was silent and did not affect the collective. This raised ambiguities between individual and collective forms of idiocy and made me reflect on the role of the designer in creating conditions for what may appear as silent withdrawals, to contribute to collective moments.

Communication devices at Occupy failed to consider what might be deviations to how participation was scripted into the modes of assembly presented. I consider that observing faltering attempts to faithful communication—which might be even described as unsuccessful in some cases—may actually allow opportunities for miscommunication to be carefully explored and can open new insights where subversion, mishaps, hesitations, silences and tactical responses have the potential to create new political formations. But these ask for a change of positioning in designing communication; a change that involves an ethopolitical engagement that recasts communication design and the qualities of participation brought into a communicative arena. In this more permeable and complex understanding of a design context, participation becomes an open, shared, speculative process of negotiation, nuanced by the subjective and affected position of the designer, by considering diverse types of participation—brought for example by human and non human partakers—and new inhabitations of communication that expand on what it means to participate in a communicative arena.

For a communication designer, taking on miscommunication is not easy, because miscommunication design demands a move towards challenging readings of contexts and situations and making the political choice of allowing questions brought by what is exterior to faithful communication to reshape practices. This view implies that communication should not be limited to general levels of the political, but should create other modalities of exchange, affects, performances of communication that call on diverse ways of being and becoming public. In an approach to communication design that is open to trial, to error and risk; to creating new communicative arenas and political formations; an approach that is speculative and explores miscommunication as a productive part of communication.

BIBLIOGRAPHY

Adams, Thije. *Kunst als publiek goed: Een pleidooi voor de culturele dimensie van een vrije samenleving.* Amsterdam: Van Gennep, 2013.

Agamben, Giorgio. *Profanations.* Translated by Jeff Fort. New York: Zone Books, 2007.

Althusser, Louis. *Lenin and Philosophy and Other Essays.* Translated by Ben Brewster. New York: Monthly Review Press, 2001 (1st ed. 1971).

Arendt, Hannah. *The Human Condition.* Chicago and London: University of Chicago Press, 1958 (2nd ed., 1998).

Argyropoulou, Gigi. 'Embros: Twelve Thoughts on the Rise and Fall of Performance Practice on the Periphery of Europe.' *Performance Research* 17, no. 6 (2012), pp. 65–62.

Bataille, Georges. *The Accursed Share: An Essay on General Economy.* Translated by Robert Hurley. New York: Zone Books, 1988. Originally published as *La Part maudit: Essay d'économie générale* (Paris: Éditions du Minuit, 1949).

Beauvallet, Ève. 'La scène indé essaime à Athènes.' *Libération,* 28 January 2016, next.liberation.fr/theatre/2016/01/28/la-scene-inde-essaime-a-athenes_1429621

Bellacasa, Maria Puig de la. 'Matters of Care in Technoscience: Assembling Neglected Things.' *Social Studies of Science* 41, no. 1 (2011), pp. 85-106.

Benkler, Yochai. *The Wealth of Networks: How Social Production Transforms Markets and Freedom.* New Haven, CO: Yale University Press, 2006.

Black, Bob. *The Abolition of Work and Other Essays.* Port Townsend, WA: Loompanics Unlimited, 1986.

Blisset, Luther (pseud.). 'H aigli tis koinotitas sti sygxroni techni: Ta "koina" kai I eksotikopoiisi tis antistasis.' ['The glamor of community in contemporary art: The "commons" and the exoticization of resistance']. *Kritiki + Techni* 5 (2013), pp.78–90.

Bockma, Harmen. 'Halbe Zijlstra: "Er zit pijn in de bezuinigingen, dat klopt".' *de Volkskrant,* 11 June 2011. www.volkskrant.nl/binnenland/halbe-zijlstra-er-zit-pijn-in-de-bezuinigingen-dat-klopt~a2444187/ (accessed 7 April 2016).

Boekman, Emanuel. *Overheid en kunst in Nederland.* PhD diss., University of Amsterdam, 1939 (reprinted 1989).

Boomgaard, Jeroen. *Wild Park: Commissioning the Unexpected.* Amsterdam: Netherlands Foundation for Visual Arts, Design and Architecture, 2011.

Bourriaud, Nicolas. *Relational Aesthetics.* Translated by Simon Pleasance and Fronza Woods with Mathieu Copeland. Dijon: Les presses du réel, 2002.

Cilliers, Paul. *Complexity and Postmodernism: Understanding Complex Systems.* London: Routledge, 1998.

Colander, David, and Roland Kupers. *Complexity and the Art of Public Policy: Solving Society's Problems from the Bottom Up.* Princeton: Princeton University Press, 2014.

Davidts, Wouter. 'The Vast and the Void On Tate Modern's Turbine Hall
     and "The Unilever Series".' *Footprint: Delft Architecture Theory Journal* 1
     (Autumn 2007), pp. 77-92.
Debord, Guy. 'Preface to *Potlatch (1954–57)*.' Translated by Reuben
     Keehan. November 1985, www.cddc.vt.edu/sionline/postsi/
     potlatchpreface.html (accessed 7 November 2016). Originally
     published in *Potlatch: 1954–57* (Paris: Gérard Lebovici, 1985).
Deleuze, Gilles, and Félix Guattari. *What Is Philosophy?* Translated by
     Graham Burchell and Hugh Tomlinson. London and Brooklyn: Verso,
     2009, 2nd ed. Originally published as *Qu'est-a que la philosophie?*
     (Paris: Éditions de Minuit, 1991).
Derrida, Jacques. *Margins of Philosophy.* Translated by Alan Bass.
     Brighton: The Harvester Press, 1982.
Donadio, Rachel. 'Greece's Big Debt Drama Is a Muse for Its Artists.'
     New York Times, 14 October 2011, www.nytimes.com/2011/10/15/
     arts/in-athens-art-blossoms-amid-debt-crisis.html?scp
     =3&sq=rachel+donadio+&st=nyt%3C/a%3E%3C/p%3E&_r=1.
Doulos, Nikos, and Eva Fotiadi, eds. *Event as Process: Cities in a State
     of Emergency and the Artists' Stance*, 2013. Online reader for the 4th
     Athens Biennale AGORA, athensbiennale.org/en/agora_en/
     about-en/.athensbiennale.org/event-as-process/.
Droitcour, Brian. 'The Perils of Post-Internet Art.' *Art in America* 102, no. 10
     (November 2014), p. 110, www.artinamericamagazine.com/news-
     features/magazine/the-perils-of-post-internet-art/.
Fotiadi, Eva. 'State Interventions in Public Space in Athens and the
     Mediatization of the Crisis: Sustaining the Unsustainable Using
     Precarity as a Tool.' *European Journal for Cultural Studies* 19, no. 6
     (November 2016), pp. 708–23 (First published online 13 August 2015).
Foucault, Michel. 'The Confession of the Flesh' (1977). In *Power/
     Knowledge: Selected Interviews and Other Writings 1972–1977*. Edited
     by Colin Gordon, translated by Colin Gordon et al., pp. 194-228. New
     York: The Harvester Press, 1980.
Gielen, Pascal. 'Performing the Common City: On the Crossroads of Art,
     Politics and Public Life.' In *Interrupting the City: Artistic Constitutions
     of the Public Sphere*. Edited by Sander Bax, Pascal Gielen, Bram
     Ieven, pp. 275–99. Amsterdam: Valiz, 2015.
Gielen, Pascal, and Paul De Bruyne. *Being an Artist in Post-Fordist Times.*
     Rotterdam: NAi Publishers, 2009.
Goudouna, Sozita. 'Contemporary Greek Art: Impoverishment of Means
     Versus Abundance of Intentions.' *Journal of Poverty* 18, no. 1 (2014),
     pp. 82–102.
Gladwell, Malcolm. 'Thresholds of Violence: How School Shootings
     Catch On.' *The New Yorker*, 19 October 2015, www.newyorker.com/
     magazine/2015/10/19/thresholds-of-violence.
Goldsmith, Kenneth. 'Kenneth Goldsmith on the Joy of Acquiring Music
     via File Sharing Networks.' *Epiphanies: Life-Changing Encounters
     with Music*. Edited by Tony Herrington, p. 75. London: Strange
     Attractor, 2015.

Graeber, David. 'Occupy Wall Street's Anarchist Roots.' In *The Occupy Handbook*. Edited by Janet Byrne, pp. 141-49. New York: Back Bay Books, 2012.

Granovetter, Mark. 'Threshold Models of Collective Behavior.' *American Journal of Sociology* 83, no. 6 (May 1978), pp. 1420–43.

Habermas, Jürgen. *The Structural Transformation of the Public Sphere: An Inquiry into a Category of Bourgeois Society (Studies in Contemporary German Social Thought)*. Translated by Thomas Burger with Frederik Lawrence. Cambridge: The MIT Press, 1991. Originally published as *Strukturwandel der Öffentlichkeit*. (Neuwied: Hermann Luchterhand Verlag, 1962)

Hammenecker, Leen, Katrien Laenen, and An Seurinck, eds. *Meer dan object: Pilootprojecten Kunst in Opdracht*. Brussel: Team Vlaams Bouwmeester, 2015.

Hardin, Garrett. 'The Tragedy of the Commons.' *Science* 162, no. 3859 (13 December 1968), pp. 1243–48.

Hardt, Michael, and Antonio Negri. *Multitude: War and Democracy in the Age of Empire*, London: Penguin, 2004.

Harcourt, Bernard E. 'Political Disobedience.' *Critical Inquiry* 39, no. 1 (Autumn 2012), 33–55.

Jackson, Shannon. *Social Works: Performing Art, Supporting Publics*. New York etc.: Routledge, 2011.

Karaba, Elpida. 'Tactics of Resistance.' *Third Text* 27, no. 5 (2013), pp. 674-88.

Kellein, Thomas. *The Dream of Fluxus: George Maciunas: An Artist's Biography*. Stuttgart: Hansjörg Mayer, 2007.

Keynes, John Maynard. 'Economic Possibilities for Our Grandchildren.' In *Essays in Persuasion (1933)*, pp. 321–32. Berlin: Springer, 2010.

Kimmelman, Michael. 'Tahrir to Zuccotti, the Power of Place: Protesters, and Cities, Find Unity by Sharing Common Ground.' *The New York Times*, 23 October 2011.

Kluitenberg, Eric. *Legacies of Tactical Media: The Tactics of Occupation: From Tompkins Square to Tahrir*. (Network Notebooks; 05). Edited by Geert Lovink and Sabine Niederer. Amsterdam: Institute of Network Cultures, 2011.

Kooke, Sandra, and Henny de Lange. '"Een museum is geen stiltezone: Dan denk ik: koop dan zelf een Rembrandt".' *Trouw*, 21 April 2015, www.trouw.nl/tr/nl/4512/Cultuur/article/ detail/3971030/2015/04/21/Een-museum-is-geen- stiltezone-Dan-denk-ik-koop-dan-zelf-een-Rembrandt. dhtml (accessed 7 April 2016)

Kunst, Bojana. *Artist at Work. Proximity of Art and Capitalism*. Winchester and Washington: Zero Books, 2015.

Kurczynski, Karen. *The Art and Politics of Asger Jorn: The Avant-Garde Won't Give Up*. Farnham, Surrey and Burlington, VT: Ashgate, 2014.

Laermans, Rudi. 'Het heden van het verleden: Over ervaring en traditie, erfgoed en canonisering.' *De Witte Raaf* 178 (November-December 2015), n.p., www.dewitteraaf.be/artikel/detail/nl/4193.

Latour, Bruno. *An Inquiry into Modes of Existence*. Cambridge, MA: Harvard University Press, 2013.

Lessig, Lawrence. *Free Culture: How Big Media Uses Technology and the Law to Lock down Culture and Control Creativity*. New York: Penguin Press, 2004.

Lippard, Lucy R. *Six Years: The Dematerialization of the Art Object from 1966 to 1972*. New York and London: Praeger Publishers, 1973.

Lodewijks, Bart. *Heimwee naar krijt: Over de kronkelige weg naar krijttekeningen in Vlaanderen en Rio de Janeiro*. Amsterdam: Mondriaanfonds, 2014.

Luhmann, Niklas. *Essays on Self-Reference*. New York: Columbia University, 1990.

Maciunas, George. 'Fluxmanifesto' (1971) ('Manifesto II'). 24 February 2010, georgemaciunas.com/about/cv/manifesto-ii/ (accessed 12 July 2016).

Manuel, Pedro. 'History.' randomassociates.blogspot.nl/2011/03/blog-post_01.html.

Marlet, Gerard. *De aantrekkelijke stad: Moderne locatietheorieën en de aantrekkingskracht van Nederlandse steden*. Nijmegen: VOC Uitgevers, 2009.

Mauss, Marcel. *Essai sur le don: The Gift. Forms and Functions of Exchange in Archaic Societies*. Translated by Ian Cunnison. London: Cohen & West, 1954.

Meyer, Robinson. '90% of Wikipedia's Editors Are Male—Here's What They're Doing About It.' *The Atlantic* 25 October 2013, www.theatlantic.com/technology/archive/2013/10/90-of-wikipedias-editors-are-male-heres-what-theyre-doing-about-it/280882/ (accessed 7 November 2016).

Ministerie van CRM (Ministry of CRM), *Discussienota Kunstbeleid*. The Hague 1972.

Mitchell, William J.T. 'Image, Space, Revolution: The Arts of Occupation.' *Critical Inquiry* 39, no. 1 (Autumn 2012), pp. 8–32.

Mokoena, Thshepo. 'Tate Modern's Carnival: All the Fun – With Added Turbine Power.' *The Guardian*, 21 August 2014, www.theguardian.com/culture/2014/aug/21/tate-modern-notting-hill-carnival-event-turbine-hall.

Mouffe, Chantal. 'Public Spaces and Democratic Politics.' In *Highrise: Common Ground: Art and the Amsterdam Zuidas Area*. Edited by Jeroen Boomgaard, pp. 134–79. Amsterdam: Valiz, 2008.

Niermann, Ingo. *The Future of Art: A Manual*. Berlin: Sternberg Press, 2011.

Ostrom, Elinor. 'The Challenge of Common-Pool Resources.' *Environment: Science and Policy for Sustainable Development* July/August 2008, www.environmentmagazine.org/Archives/Back%20Issues/July-August%202008/ostrom-full.html (accessed 7 November 2016).

Panagiotara, Betina, and Steriani Tsintziloni. 'A Shifting Landscape: Contemporary Greek Dance and Conditions of Crisis.' *Journal of Greek Media & Culture* 1, no. 1 (1 April 2015), pp. 29–45.

Petropoulou, Christy. '"Alternative Networks of Collectivities" and "Solidarity Cooperative Economy" in Greek Cities: Exploring Their Theoretical Origins.' *Journal of Regional Socio-Economic Issues* 3, no. 2 (June 2013), pp. 61–86. www.jrsei.yolasite.com/resources/ Journal__Volume--III__Issue--II__2013__Online.pdf.

Petropoulou, Christy. 'Crisis, Right to the City Movements and the Question of Spontaneity: Athens and Mexico City.' *City: Analysis of Urban Trends, Culture, Theory, Policy, Action* 18, no. 4–5 (2014), pp. 563–72.

Pots, Roel. *Cultuur, koningen en democraten: Overheid & cultuur in Nederland.* Nijmegen: Boom, 2002.

Pots, Roel. 'De tijdloze Thorbecke: Over niet-oordelen en voorwaarden scheppen in het Nederlandse cultuurbeleid.' *Boekman: tijdschrift voor kunst, cultuur en beleid* 21, no. 81 (Winter 2009) (Kunst en politiek), pp. 2–14.

Price, Greg. 'How Much Does The Internet Cost To Run?' *Forbes* 14 March 2012. www.forbes.com/sites/quora/2012/03/14/how-much-does-the-internet-cost-to-run/ (accessed 7 November 2016).

Rancière, Jacques. The Politics of Aesthetics: The Distribution of the Sensible. Translated by Gabriel Rockhill. London and New York: Continuum, 2004. Originally published as Le partage du sensible: Esthétique et politique (Paris: La Fabrique, 2000).

— 'Aesthetic Separation, Aesthetic Community.' In *The Emancipated Spectator.* Translated by Gregory Elliott, pp. 51–83. London: Verso, 2009. Originally published as Le spectateur émancipé (Paris: La Fabrique, 2008) (2009a).

— 'Aesthetics as Politics.' In *Aesthetics and its Discontents.* Translated by Steven Corcoran, pp. 19–44. Cambridge, MA: Polity, 2009 (2009b).

— 'The Emancipated Spectator.' In *The Emancipated Spectator.* Translated by Gregory Elliott, pp. 1–23. London: Verso, 2009. Originally published as *Le spectateur émancipé* (Paris: La Fabrique, 2008) (2009c).

— *Dissensus. On Politics and Aesthetics.* London and New York: Continuum, 2010.

Raymond, Eric S. 'Homesteading the Noosphere.' *First Monday* 3, no. 10 (October 1998). firstmonday.org/ojs/index.php/fm/article/ view/621 (accessed 7 November 2016).

Rebentisch, Juliane. *Die Kunst der Freiheit: Zur Dialektik demokratischer Existenz.* Berlin: Suhrkamp, 2012.

Rifkin, Jeremy. *The End of Work: The Decline of the Global Labour Force and the Dawn of the Post-Market Era.* New York: Putnam, 1996.

— *The Third Industrial Revolution: How Lateral Power Is Transforming Energy, the Economy, and the World.* New York: Palgrave Macmillan, 2011.

— *The Zero Marginal Cost Society: The Internet of Things, the Collaborative Commons, and the Eclipse of Capitalism.* New York: Palgrave Macmillan, 2014.

Schinkel, Willem. 'What Do We Do When We Say: 'This Is an Artistic

Event?' A Response to Heinich.' *Boekmancahier* no. 46 (December 2000), pp. 404–13.

Segal, David. 'Swiss Freeports Are Home for a Growing Treasury of Art.' *The New York Times* 21 July 2012. www.nytimes.com/2012/07/22/business/swiss-freeports-are-home-for-a-growing-treasury-of-art.html (accessed 7 November 2016).

Sheikh, Simon. 'A Long Walk to the Land of the People: Contemporary Art in the Spectre of Spectatorship.' In *Future Publics (The Rest Can and Should Be Done by the People): A Critical Reader in Contemporary Art*. Edited by Maria Hlavajova and Ranjit Hoskote. Utrecht: BAK; Amsterdam: Valiz Publishers, 2015.

Srnicek, Nick, and Alex Williams. '# Accelerate: Manifesto for an Accelerationist Politics.' *Accelerate: The Accelerationist Reader*. Edited Robin Mackay and Armen Avanessian, pp. 347–62. Falmouth: Urbanomic, 2013.

— *Inventing the Future: Postcapitalism and a World without Work*. London: Verso, 2015.

Stengers, Isabelle. 'Introductory Notes on an Ecology of Practices.' *Cultural Studies Review* 11, no. 1 (March 2005), pp. 183–96 (2005a).

— 'The Cosmopolitical Proposal.' In *Making Things Public: Atmospheres of Democracy*. Edited by Bruno Latour and Peter Weibel, pp. 994–1003. Cambridge, MA: MIT Press, 2005 (2005b).

— 'Introductory Notes on an Ecology of Practices.' *Cultural Studies Review* 11, no. 1 (March 2005), 183–96 (2005c).

— 'Experimenting with Refrains: Subjectivity and the Challenge of Escaping Modern Dualism.' *Subjectivity* 22 (2008), pp. 38–59.

Taussig, Michael. 'I'm So Angry I Made a Sign.' *Critical Inquiry* 39, no. 1 (Autumn 2012), pp. 56–88.

Tsiara, Syrago. 'Contemporary Greek Art in Times of Crisis: Cuts and Changes.' *Journal of Visual Culture* 14, no. 2 (1 August 2015), pp. 176–81.

Vaiou, Dina, and Ares Kalandides. 'Practices of Collective Action and Solidarity: Reconfigurations of the Public Space in Crisis-Ridden Athens, Greece.' *Journal of Housing and the Built Environment* 31, no. 3 (2015), pp. 457–70. Online first 26 July 2015. link.springer.com/article/10.1007%2Fs10901-015-9468-z#/page-1 (accessed 18 February 2016).

Van den Dool, Pim. 'Onderzoek NRC: brede steun voor kunstbeleid Zijlstra.' *NRC Handelsblad*, 3 September 2011, www.nrc.nl/nieuws/2011/09/03/onderzoek-nrc-brede-steun-voor-kunstbeleid-zijlstra (accessed 7 April 2016).

Vidal, John. 'Health Risks of Shipping Pollution Have Been "Underestimated".' *The Guardian*, 9 April 2009. www.theguardian.com/environment/2009/apr/09/shipping-pollution (accessed 7 November 2016).

Virno, Paolo. *A Grammar of the Multitude: For an Analysis of Contemporary Forms of Life*. Cambridge, MA and London: Harvard University Press, 2004.

Von Osten, Marion, et al. 'She Now Works Flexible.' In *Taking the Matter into Common Hands*. Edited by Johanna Billing, Maria Lind and Lars Nilsson, p. 69. London: Black Dog, 2007.

Wanders, Gijs. *Gezichten van dementie*. Zwolle: Wbooks, 2013.

Wegerif, Anne. *Ontwikkeling in de belangstelling voor musea: De cultuurparticipatie van de Nederlandse bevolking in de periode 1950 tot 2005 toegespits op musea nader onderzocht*. PhD diss., Erasmus University Rotterdam, 2008. file:///Users/steven/Downloads/Masterthesis%20(2).pdf (accessed 7 April 2016).

Zantingh, Peter. 'Topinstellingen worden gespaard bij cultuurbezuinigingen.' *NRC Handelsblad*, 10 June 2011, www.nrc.nl/nieuws/2011/06/10/topinstellingen-worden-gespaard-bij-cultuurbezuinigingen (accessed 7 April 2016).

Zuidervaart, Lambert. *Art in Public: Politics, Economics, and a Democratic Culture*. Cambridge: Cambridge University Press, 2011.

WEBSITES

Ahmed, Tarif. 'Why I Occupy: A Boston University Undergratuate Explains.' 24 October 2011, www.thenation.com/article/why-i-occupy.

Athens Biennale. 'The Athens Biennale 2015–2017 "OMONOIA" begins its official programme on 18 November 2015 with Synapse 1.' 15 November 2015, athensbiennale.org/en/news/the-athens-biennale-2015-2017-%CE%BF%CE%BC%CE%BF%CE%BD%CE%BF%CE%B9%CE%B1-begins-its-official-programme-on-18-november-2015-with-synapse-1/ (accessed 18 February 2016).

Athens Biennale Kyklos, athensbiennale.org/en/agora_en/kyklos_en/ (accessed 18 February 2016). www.auerfeld.com/images/occupyewleaflet.pdf.

Barbrook, Richard. 'The Hi-Tech Gift Economy.' *First Monday* special issue 3 (5 December 2005), firstmonday.org/article/viewArticle/1517/1432 (accessed 7 November 2016).

Batista, Elysa D. 'OWS Sign Language.' #searchunderoccupy, searchunderoccupy.parsons.edu/ows-sign-language/.

Bloomberg Philanthropies. 'Five Cities Selected As Winners in Bloomberg Philanthropies 2014 Mayors Challenge.' 17 September 2014, www.bloomberg.org/press/releases/five-cities-selected-winners-bloomberg-philanthropies-2014-mayors-challenge/ (accessed 18 February 2016).

Bourdrez, Aernoud. 'Sehgal en het betreden van de leefwereld'. *Stedelijk Museum Amsterdam Journal* 27 August 2015, journal.stedelijk.nl/sehgal-en-het-betreden-van-de-leefwereld-2/#more-6276

British Library. 'Collection Items: Hobbes's Leviathan.' www.bl.uk/collection-items/hobbess-leviathan.

CBS. 'Nederlandse bevolking steeds hoger opgeleid.' 25 July 2005, www.cbs.nl/nl-nl/nieuws/2005/30/nederlandse-bevolking-steeds-hoger-opgeleid (accessed 7 April 2016).

CommonsFest 2016. commonsfest.info/en/ (accessed 14 March 2016).

Coumans, Anke, and Herman van Hoogdalem. 'Portretteren in context.'
24 February 2016, kc.academieminerva.nl/media/17367.

Dammbeck, Lutz. *The Net: The Unabomber, LSD and the Internet*. 2005 (film).

Debord, Guy. 'Potlatch (1954–57).' May 2007, www.notbored.org/
potlatch.html. Except where noted, translated from the French
from: *Guy Debord Correspondance. Vol 6: Janvier 1979–Decembre
1987* (Paris: Librairie Artheme Fayard, 2006).

Doulos, Nikos, and Eva Fotiadi, eds. *Event as Process: Cities in a State of
Emergency and the Artists' Stance.* Online reader for the 4th Athens
Biennale AGORA. 2013, athensbiennale.org/en/agora_en/
about-en/.athensbiennale.org/event-as-process/
(accessed 18 February 2016).

European Cultural Foundation 2015. *ECF Princess Margriet Award for
Culture 2015*, www.culturalfoundation.eu/pma-2015
(accessed 18 February 2016).

Free Self-managed Embros Theatre, www.embros.gr/
(accessed 18 February 2016).

Groupies, Roy. 'Arundhati Roy @ the People's University.' YouTube,
uploaded 17 November 2011.

Groys, Boris. 'Under the Gaze of Theory.' *E-flux Journal* 35 (May 2012),
www.e-flux.com/journal/35/68389/under-the-gaze-of-
theory/.

Howard, Philip N., et al. 'Opening Closed Regimes: What Was the Role of
Social Media During the Arab Spring?' 2011, dx.doi.org/10.2139/
ssrn.2595096.

'Institute for the Management of the Athenian Post-Documenta
Melancholy', 7 February 2016, idammathens.wordpress.com/
(accessed 18 February 2016).

Kelly, Tom, and Damien Gayle. 'The Thermal Images That Prove 90%
of Tents in the Occupy Camp in London Are Left Empty Overnight.'
Mail Online 26 October 2011, www.dailymail.co.uk/news/
article-2053463/Occupy-London-90-tents-St-Pauls-
protest-camp-left-overnight.html

Koebler, Jason. 'The Secret Search Engine Tearing Wikipedia Apart.'
Motherboard 15 February 2016, motherboard.vice.com/read/
wikipedias-secret-google-competitor-search-engine-is-
tearing-it-apart (accessed 7 November 2016).

Kuhnt, Sarah. 'Beyond the Crisis: On Greece's Burgeoning Art Scene.'
Afterall/Online 4 July 2012, www.afterall.org/online/beyond-
the-crisis-on-greece-s-burgeoning-contemporary-art-
scene#.VuiUoXpSJUA.

'Linus Torvalds Wins Prix Ars Electronica Golden Nica.' *Linux Today*
29 May 1999, www.linuxtoday.com/news/1999052900305PS
(accessed 7 November 2016).

[MacGraw], Sheila. 'Embros Theatre: Addressing cultural demolition
in Athens with temporary interventions.' *New Europes. Cities in
Transition*, 2 February 2015, citiesintransition.eu/place/
embros-theatre.

Maciunas, George. 'Manifesto II.' [1971]. 2010,
    georgemaciunas.com/about/cv/manifesto-ii/
    (accessed 12 July 2016).

Mansoux, Aymeric. 'My Lawyer Is an Artist: Free Culture Licenses as
    Art Manifestos.' *Hz: Fylkingen's Web Journal* 19 (2014), www.hz-
    journal.org/n19/mansoux.html (accessed 7 November 2016).

Manuel, Pedro. 'History.' 2011, randomassociates.blogspot.
    nl/2011/03/blog-post_01.html.

Mansoux, Aymeric. 'My Lawyer Is an Artist: Free Culture Licenses as
    Art Manifestos.' *Hz: Fylkingen's Web Journal* 19 (2014), www.hz-
    journal.org/n19/mansoux.html (accessed 7 November 2016).

Mavili Collective. 2014, mavilicollective.wordpress.com/.

Mavili Collective. 2012, kinisimavili.blogspot.de/p/1-4-2011-
    2012.html.

Merriam-Webster. 'Definition of PUBLIC DOMAIN.' 2016, www.merriam-
    webster.com/dictionary/public+domain (accessed 7 November
    2016).

Musea. 'Infographic: Nederlandse musea 2015 in kaart gebracht.' 2015,
    www.em-cultuur.nl/nieuws/infographics/nederlandse-
    musea-2015-in-kaart-gebracht/ (accessed 7 April 2016).

Netpol. 'Guide to "Kettles".' Netpol: The Network for Police Monitoring,
    netpol.org/guide-to-kettles/.

OCCUPYLSX. *A Toolkit for Occupy Everywhere.* 2011, occupywallst.org/.

'Open Call: Athens Biennale 2013 Agora.' 2013, athensbiennale.org/
    en/agora_en/open_call_en/ (accessed 18 February 2016).

Papadopoulos, Dimitris, Vassilis Tsianos and Margarita Tsomou.
    'Athens: Metropolitan Blockade: Real Democracy.' *Transversal*
    (July 2012), eipcp.net/transversal/1011/ptt/en.

Rancière, Jacques. 'The Politics of Aesthetics.' *Mute* 14 September 2006,
    www.metamute.org/editorial/articles/politics-aesthetics.

— 'Aesthetic Separation, Aesthetic Community: Scenes from the
    Aesthetic Regime of Art.' *Art & Research: A Journal of Ideas, Contexts
    and Methods* 2, no. 1 (Summer 2008), n.p.,
    www.artandresearch.org.uk/v2n1/pdfs/ranciere.pdf.

Rey, P.J. 'Why We Disrupt.' *Inside Higher ED*, www.insidehighered.
    com/views/2012/01/03/essay-why-occupy-movement-
    disrupts-speakers-campus – sthash.pf9hun5M.dpbs.

'Ruim 400.000 bezoekers, maar ook honderden klachten over drukte in
    Rijks.' AT5, 2015, www.at5.nl/artikelen/142304/ruim_400000_
    bezoekers_maar_ook_honderden_klachten_over_drukte_
    in_rijks (accessed 7 April 2016).

Spreeuwenberg, Kimberley, and Thomas Poell. 'Android and the Political
    Economy of the Mobile Internet: A Renewal of Open Source Critique.'
    First Monday 17, no. 7 (July 2012), firstmonday.org/ojs/index.
    php/fm/article/view/4050 (accessed 7 November 2016).

Steyerl, Hito. 'Too Much World: Is the Internet Dead?' *e-flux journal* 49
    (2013), www.e-flux.com/journal/49/60004/too-much-world-
    is-the-internet-dead/ (accessed 7 November 2016).

SynAthina, www.synathina.gr/ (accessed 18 February 2016).

Yegulalp, Serdar. 'Who Writes Linux? Corporations, More than Ever.' *InfoWorld*, 3 February 2014, www.infoworld.com/article/2610207/ open-source-software/who-writes-linux-corporations-more-than-ever.html (accessed 7 November 2016).

INDEX OF NAMES

CONTRIBUTORS

JEROEN BOOMGAARD (born 1953) holds a PhD in art history from the University of Amsterdam. He is Professor of Art and Public Space at the Gerrit Rietveld Academie Amsterdam. He is also head of the research master's programme Artistic Research at the University of Amsterdam. His recent publications include *Wild Park: Commissioning the Unexpected* (2011) and the co-editing of *Open* magazine's issue *Politics of Things: What Art & Design Do in Democracy* (2012).

Boomgaard lives and works in Amsterdam.

ROGIER BROM (born 1982) is a freelance art historian and art sociologist who studied at Utrecht University and Erasmus University Rotterdam. He researches how art and its public make contact, as well as the consequences of the circumstances within which this contact takes place. He is also a member of the LAPS knowledge network, the Research Institute for Art & Public Space at the Gerrit Rietveld Academie Amsterdam and works at the Centraal Museum Utrecht.

Besides teaching art history at several institutes, his projects include: *Art with an assignment* (2016–2017), in which he develops a method to assess the appreciation of art in public space, and *Scan HKU* (2015–2016), scanning the position of research in the curriculum of the HKU University of the Arts Utrecht.

Brom lives and works in Amsterdam.

ANKE COUMANS (born 1962) studied philosophy, film theory and semiotics. She holds a PhD from Leiden University with a thesis on artistic, public communication titled 'Can an image say I'. Since 2012 she is professor Image in Context at the Research Centre Art & Society at Minerva Art Academy in Groningen. Her research concerns the intermingling and influencing of the domains of art practice, social practice and research practice. She is also connected to HKU University of the Arts where, together with Ingrid Schuffelers, she developed the interdisciplinary learning communities Membrane and Golgi. In these environments students, teachers and partners find new roles in innovative artistic practices.

Recent exhibitions she organized include *We, People in transition* (producer and curator), Minerva Platform, Groningen (2016) and *You and me and everyone we do not know* (producer), Minerva Platform, Groningen (2016). Recent articles include: 'Reflections on Artist Organisations International', *Open!* (June 2015), www.onlineopen.org/reflections-on-artist-organisations-international,

'Vervreemding als strategie', *de Helling* (Summer 2015), 'Alienation as Strategy of Political Artists: A Reflection on the Work of the Political Artists from Artist Organization International', www.academia.edu/26852097/Alienation_as_strategy_of_political_artists.docx,

'Kunst en propaganda, twee recente voorbeelden uit Istanbul', www.academia.edu/5067191/Kunst_en_propaganda_twee_recente_voorbeelden_uit_Istanbul, 'Vervreemding als politiek interventie', *Filosofie & Praktijk* (Autumn 2012), www.academia.edu/2365581/vervreemding_als_politieke_interventie.

Coumans lives in Slijk-Ewijk and works in Utrecht and Groningen.

FLORIAN CRAMER (born 1969) is a participant observer of experimental arts. He studied comparative literature and art history at Freie Universität Berlin, Universität Konstanz and University of Massachusetts at Amherst and is a reader in 21st-century visual culture at the Creating 010 Research Centre of Rotterdam University of Applied Sciences, where he is affiliated to Willem de Kooning Academy and Piet Zwart Institute, Rotterdam. His recent publications include 'What Is "Post-Digital"?', *APRJA Journal* (2014), and *Anti-Media: Ephemera on Speculative Arts* (2013).

Cramer lives and works in Rotterdam.

EVA FOTIADI (born 1977) is an art historian. In 2014–2016 she was a full-time research fellow at Freie Universität Berlin and Princeton University, writing about collective actions and events in Athens since 2000. Her current project's publications include 'History-Space-Memory-Body: Artists' Performative Interventions in the Refugee Houses on Alexandra's Avenue in Athens' (forthcoming 2017), *JMGS*, 'State Interventions in Public Space in Athens and the Mediatization of the Crisis', *EJCS* (2015); and the co-editing of the online reader *Event as Process: Cities in an Ongoing State of Emergency and the Artists' Stance* (2013) for the 4th Athens Biennial.

Fotiadi lives and works in Berlin and Amsterdam.

MAAIKE LAUWAERT (born 1978) is a writer and researcher who studied cultural sciences and is currently head of internal affairs at de Appel arts centre in Amsterdam. Since 2000, she writes about contemporary art in the Netherlands and abroad in magazines, books and on websites, including *Metropolis M*, *De Witte Raaf*, *Kaleidoscope*, and *Artforum*. Her research projects into artists initiatives and the financial situation of visual artists were valued in the arts field and picked up by policy makers. As a freelance curator she was involved with, among other projects, *Kaap 2014* and since 2013 she works for the foundation Kunst in het Stationsgebied, which realized the *Call of the Mall* exhibition. Before she started as an editor for *Metropolis M*, she worked as visual arts curator at Stroom Den Haag, was project officer at the Mondriaan Foundation and obtained a PhD at the Faculty of Arts and Social Sciences of Maastricht University. She was co-editor of *Facing Value: Radical Perspectives from the Arts* (2017).

Lauwaert lives and works in Amsterdam.

GABRIEL LESTER (born 1972) is an artist and filmmaker. His artworks, films/videos, performances and installations originate from a desire to tell stories and construct environments that support these stories or propose their own narrative interpretation. Other activities include commissioned artworks for the public space, film directing, teaching and writing.

Selected solo exhibitions: *The Nine Day Week*, CAC, Vilnius (2016), *Apple Z*, de Appel arts centre, Amsterdam (2016), *The Ears Have Walls*, Leo Xu Projects, Shanghai (2014), *Suspension of Disbelief*, Museum Boijmans Van Beuningen, Rotterdam (2011). Selected group exhibitions: *Forming in the Pupil of an Eye*, Kochi Biennale (2016), Moscow Biennale (2015), Istanbul Biennale (2015), CAFA Museum, Beijing (2014), Venice Biennale (2013).

Lester lives and works in Amsterdam.

BARBARA NEVES ALVES (born 1974) is a designer and researcher. In 2016 she obtained a PhD with the thesis 'Miscommunicating and design: researching miscommunication as a proposition for designing political scenes' at the Design department at Goldsmiths, University of London. Her current research interests and areas of work include ecologies of communication, politics of communication, noise, participatory methods, emerging modes of practice.

With a background in communication design, type design and typography, she has worked in a variety of settings and places, and remained regularly active as a lecturer in higher education. In the past few years she has focused on a practice-based research into communication design within socially and politically engaged modes of practice.

Neves Alves lives and works in Amsterdam.

STEVEN TEN THIJE (born 1980) studied art history and philosophy at the University of Amsterdam. Currently he works as project leader for *The Uses of Art*, on the legacy of 1848 and 1989, a five-year project by L'Internationale, a confederation of six European heritage institutes focused on modern and contemporary art and culture. In the programme he is active on the editorial board of L'Internationale Online (www.internationaleonline.org) and he co-curated *Confessions of the Imperfect, 1848–1989–Today* (Van Abbemuseum, Eindhoven, 2014–2015). He was part of the editorial team of the publication *What's the Use?*

Constellations of Art, History and Knowledge (2016). In the first L'Internationale project on post-war avant-gardes he was part of the curatorial team of *Spirits of Internationalism* (Van Abbemuseum, Eindhoven and M HKA, Antwerp, 2012). He recently published the Mondriaan Fund's essay *Het geëmancipeerde museum* ('The emancipated museum') (2016). He has written various articles and reviews in publications such *as Exhibiting the New Art: 'Op Losse Schroeven' and 'When Attitudes Become Form' 1969* (2010).

Ten Thije lives and works in Eindhoven.

CONTRIBUTORS

COLOPHON

Editors: Jeroen Boomgaard, Rogier Brom
Authors: Jeroen Boomgaard, Rogier Brom,
Anke Coumans, Florian Cramer, Eva Fotiadi,
Maaike Lauwaert, Gabriel Lester,
Barbara Neves Alves, Steven ten Thije
Editorial assistance: Sietske Roorda,
Sarah van Binsbergen, Pia Pol
Translation and copy-editing: Leo Reijnen
Proofreading: Els Brinkman
Index: Elke Stevens
Production: Sarah van Binsbergen

Graphic design: Template,
www.template01.info
Typefaces: Tex Gyre Bonum,
Tex Gyre Chorus
Paper inside: Munken Print White, 100 gr
Paper cover: Bioset 240 gr
Printing: Bariet-Ten Brink, Meppel

Publisher: Astrid Vorstermans,
Valiz, Amsterdam
Amsterdam, 2017

Valiz, Amsterdam
www.valiz.nl
LAPS, Research Institute for Art
and Public Space
www.laps-rietveld.nl
Gerrit Rietveld Academie,
Amsterdam
www.rietveldacademie.nl

The editors and the publisher have made every
effort to secure permission to reproduce the
listed material, texts and illustrations. We apolo-
gize for any inadvert errors or omissions. Parties
who nevertheless believe they can claim specific
legal rights are invited to contact the publisher.
info@valiz.nl

ISBN 978-94-92095-28-2
Printed and bound in the EU

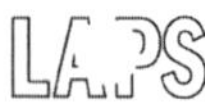

Gerrit Rietveld Academie

INTERNATIONAL DISTRIBUTION
BE/NL/LU: Coen Sligting,
www.coensligtingbookimport.nl;
Centraal Boekhuis,
www.centraal.boekhuis.nl
GB/IE: Anagram Books,
www.anagrambooks.com
Europe (excl GB/IE)/Asia:
Idea Books, www.ideabooks.nl
Australia: Perimeter,
www.perimeterdistribution.com
USA, Canada, Latin-America: D.A.P.,
www.artbook.com
Individual orders:
www.valiz.nl; info@valiz.nl